# Nature Poetry

## "Make Me a Picture of the Sun"

# Pure Poetry

# Nature Poetry

## "Make Me a Picture of the Sun"

**Enslow Publishers, Inc.**
40 Industrial Road
Box 398
Berkeley Heights, NJ 07922
USA

http://www.enslow.com

Sheila Griffin Llanas

**Library of Congress Cataloging-in-Publication Data**

Llanas, Sheila Griffin, 1958–

    Nature poetry : "Make me a picture of the sun" / Sheila Griffin Llanas.
        pages cm. — (Pure Poetry)
    Includes index.
    Summary: "Explores nature poetry, including famous American and European poets
      and their poems, as well as literary criticism, poetic technique, explication, and
      prompts for further study"—Provided by publisher.
    ISBN 978-0-7660-4244-5
    1. Nature—Juvenile literature. 2. Nature in literature. I. Title.
    PN6110.N2L56 2013
    808.81'936—dc23

                      2013007355

Future editions:
Paperback ISBN: 978-1-4644-0431-3
EPUB ISBN: 978-1-4645-1235-3
Single-User PDF ISBN: 978-1-4646-1235-0
Multi-User PDF ISBN: 978-0-7660-5867-5

Printed in the United States of America

112013 Lake Book Manufacturing, Inc., Melrose Park, IL

10 9 8 7 6 5 4 3 2 1

**To Our Readers:** We have done our best to make sure all Internet addresses in this
book were active and appropriate when we went to press. However, the author and the
publisher have no control over and assume no liability for the material available on those
Internet sites or on other Web sites they may link to. Any comments or suggestions can
be sent by e-mail to comments@enslow.com or to the address on the back cover.

♻ Enslow Publishers, Inc., is committed to printing our books on recycled paper. The
paper in every book contains 10% to 30% post-consumer waste (PCW). The cover board
on the outside of each book contains 100% PCW. Our goal is to do our part to help
young people and the environment too!

**Photo and Illustration Credits:** Library of Congress, pp. 42, 65, 78, 92, 102; Mary Evans
Picture Library/Everett Collection, pp. 11, 54; Photos.com/© Thinkstock, p. 25.

**Cover Illustration:** Shutterstock.com.

# Contents

# Introduction

**T**hroughout the ages, poets and artists have been sensitive to nature. The British and American poets in this volume wrote during or after the Romantic era, a time that fostered a lasting reverence for nature.

During the Romantic era, some artists and poets began to work outside. They stood in the landscapes they painted and described the scenes. In their art forms, they showed the movement of wind and water. They brought nature to life, often giving it the raw, untouched quality of wilderness.

To these wild natural settings, Romantic poets linked their own emotions and memories. They studied humanity's impact on nature and nature's impact on the human psyche. Connecting landscapes to human experiences was a very new idea. In that way, nature poems of the Romantic era often explore and reflect human nature.

# Nature Poetry: "Make Me a Picture of the Sun"

Each chapter in this book contains biographical, contextual, and analytical information about the poet and the poem. Every chapter ends with five questions. Three are short-answer questions, requiring brief responses. For help, review the text. The other two ask you to "ponder further" and look beyond the chapter, perhaps to another source, to write a longer answer.

You can also interact with any poem in general ways:

- **Study the poems.** Be patient. Read the poems slowly, a few lines at a time if necessary. Read them aloud. Remember, they are not supposed to be easy to read. To make sure you have done a close reading, write your own summary of a poem.

- **Analyze the analysis.** A good analysis is based on a close reading, but it also asserts one reader's opinion. As you read a poem's explication, decide whether you agree with it or not. Using the chapter's explication as a model, form an interpretation of your own.

- **Make a comparison.** Compare any poem to any one of the other seven poems. When you set them side by side, striking differences will appear. This helps you more clearly understand elements of each poem. Note your observations in a two-column chart or a brief essay.

- **Consider the poet.** Notice biographical details of each poet. Is the poet American or British, a man or a woman? How might these factors influence the work?

Which details in a poem reflect its author's heritage and background, gender, or social status?

When you close this book, you may find yourself thinking about the poems later. The poets represented here wrote many poems. If you feel inspired to read more, you can find their work online, in the library, or in a bookstore. And if you feel inspired to write poetry of your own, all you need is a place to write down your words.

# 1

## "To the Moon"
## Charlotte Turner Smith
### (1749–1806)

In the eighteenth century, people followed strict codes of social manners, morals, and behaviors. Women, especially, learned to hide emotions and suppress their desires. Charlotte Turner Smith wrote poetry to express her deepest feelings. At first, she kept her poems private. When she needed money to support her children, she published her work.

In her introduction to her book's sixth edition, published in 1792, Smith admitted, "I wrote mournfully because I was unhappy." She kept the source of her sadness private. She did not name the reasons for her misery, such as her unhappy marriage, financial struggles, or challenges of motherhood. Instead, Smith created personas, speakers who conveyed the emotional distress,

Charlotte Turner Smith

# Charlotte Turner Smith

Charlotte Turner Smith was born in 1749 to wealthy parents. When she was four, her mother died. She attended school in London and spent her free time in South Downs, Sussex, along the southeastern coast of England. The area features dramatic white bluffs, including Beachy Head, Britain's highest chalk sea cliff. It was a place that fed her love of natural beauty. Later, she often described this landscape in her poems.

She married young, at age fifteen, in 1765. She quickly learned she had made a mistake. Her husband was abusive and a gambler. The couple moved to London, struggled financially, and, in spite of the unhappy marriage, had twelve children, eight of whom survived.

In 1783, her husband was sent to prison for debt. At the time, family members could come and go from the jail. She lived with him in his cell. To earn money to free him, in 1784, she published *Elegiac Sonnets*.

In 1786, she left her husband and moved with her children to Brighton and West Sussex. In her lifetime, she wrote twelve novels and three volumes of poetry, as well as four educational books for young people, a natural history of birds, and a history of England. She died in 1806. She was one of the most popular writers of her time.

but not the facts, of her circumstances. Smith's first book, *Elegiac Sonnets*, first printed in 1784, became hugely popular, probably because so many women shared her thoughts and emotions.

Smith places her speakers in natural settings that are dark and bleak, almost frightening. The mood of her poems is often sorrow or despair. During the Romantic era, readers grew hungry for more of this type of literature. Gothic novels were gaining popularity—stories of mystery, suspense, and horror.

Many authors, like Smith, combined gothic elements with another new cultural interest in botany—the study of plants. Smith makes her settings seem almost haunted with lush nature imagery.

This section from "Sonnet XXII" was written near the seashore in October 1784:

> *O'er the dark waves the winds tempestuous howl;*
> *The screaming sea-bird quits the troubled sea:*
> *But the wild gloomy scene has charms for me,*
> *And suits the mournful temper of my soul.*

The speaker sits on a cliff in weather so harsh that even the birds fly away. Outer nature, the "wild gloomy scene," reflects the speaker's inner mood, her "mournful temper." Smith describes nature in ways that reflect the emotions of her speakers.

# Sonnet IV: To the Moon

*Queen of the silver bow!—by thy pale beam,*
*Alone and pensive, I delight to stray,*
*And watch thy shadow trembling in the stream,*
*Or mark the floating clouds that cross thy way.*
*And while I gaze, thy mild and placid\* light*
*Sheds a soft calm upon my troubled breast—*
*And oft I think—fair planet of the night,*
*That in thy orb, the wretched may have rest:*
*The sufferers of the earth perhaps may go,*
*Released by death—to thy benignant\* sphere,*
*And the sad children of despair and woe*
*Forget in thee, their cup of sorrow here.*
*Oh! that I soon may reach thy world serene,*
*Poor wearied pilgrim—in this toiling scene!*

\***placid:** calm, undisturbed

\***benignant:** beneficial; kindly or merciful

# Summary

The speaker in "To the Moon" wanders outside at night. She tenderly gazes up at and speaks to the moon, the "Queen of the silver bow." She watches the moon's reflection, its shadow in a stream, and clouds covering it. She does not mention anything on Earth, not even the ground on which she walks.

She walks in a moonbeam, and moonlight touches her heart. When it makes her feel calm, she enters the world of her imagination. She fantasizes that the dead go to the moon and find peace or, at least, stop suffering. Finally, she admits that she longs for the place she just dreamed of, but she must stay where she is—on Earth, in life.

# Explication

In "To the Moon," a woman has an intimate relationship with nature that only heightens her sense of loneliness. The speaker addresses the moon, her celestial companion. However, instead of taking solace from the night sky, she experiences a disconnection. Even as she speaks directly to the moon, and the moon's light touches her, other images in her poem suggest that she and the moon can never connect.

Smith engages only the sense of sight in her description. The speaker sees the moon, the clouds, and a stream. Failing to use her other senses adds to her disconnection. Earth's nature is tangible and physical. It can be felt, tasted, smelled, and heard. However, the speaker never describes anything on Earth. Although she is outside, she is unaware of any plants, grasses, trees, animals, or breezes. The mysteries of nature she speaks of in "To the Moon" are all beyond reach.

Even what she sees emphasizes her separation from the moon. The moon's shadows are a reflection, not the moon itself. Clouds over the moon heighten her separation. When she claims that the moon's light "[s]heds a soft calm upon my troubled breast," what she feels is her own nature, not the moon's. At this point, the poem changes direction. The speaker's separation from the outer scene is complete. She no longer gazes at the natural world. She turns her gaze inward, to her imagination, where she creates a fantastical purpose for the unreachable moon.

The speaker imagines the moon is the realm of the dead. It is a place where "the wretched may have rest," and the "sufferers of the Earth" could be "[r]eleased by death." The speaker never hopes the moon is a place of joy, only a place absent of suffering. It is human happiness that is unreachable in this sad, mournful poem—not the moon.

The speaker's admission in the poem's conclusion is abrupt. It may have shocked her readers. The speaker, according to her time, was supposed to accept her problems and carry on. Instead, she expresses a longing to escape her reality: "Oh! that I soon may reach thy world serene,/Poor wearied pilgrim—in this toiling scene!" The speaker knows

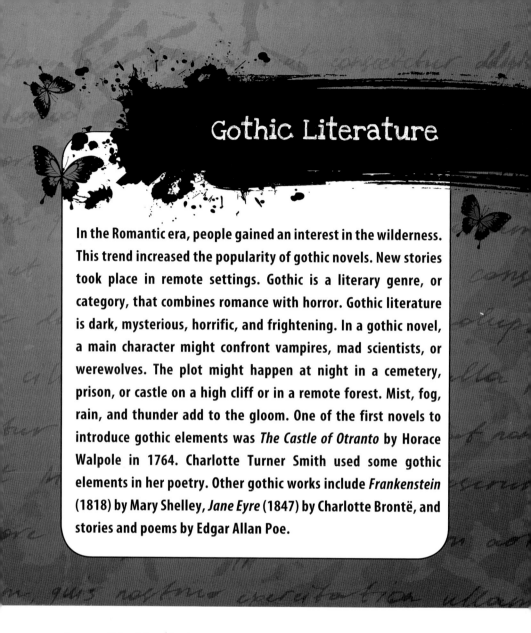

# Gothic Literature

In the Romantic era, people gained an interest in the wilderness. This trend increased the popularity of gothic novels. New stories took place in remote settings. Gothic is a literary genre, or category, that combines romance with horror. Gothic literature is dark, mysterious, horrific, and frightening. In a gothic novel, a main character might confront vampires, mad scientists, or werewolves. The plot might happen at night in a cemetery, prison, or castle on a high cliff or in a remote forest. Mist, fog, rain, and thunder add to the gloom. One of the first novels to introduce gothic elements was *The Castle of Otranto* by Horace Walpole in 1764. Charlotte Turner Smith used some gothic elements in her poetry. Other gothic works include *Frankenstein* (1818) by Mary Shelley, *Jane Eyre* (1847) by Charlotte Brontë, and stories and poems by Edgar Allan Poe.

the world of death she imagines is not real, yet she still wants to go there. She knows the impossibility of her longing.

Ultimately, the poem is not about the moon or even death. It is about living with an aching loneliness. In this poem, the moon is as unreachable from Earth as happiness is from the speaker's life.

# Style, Technique, and Poetic Devices

"To the Moon," like many of Smith's sonnets, contains the morbid elements of gothic novels that grew so popular during her time. The night landscape is ghostly with moonlight, but the speaker is untouched by the loveliness of the scene. She dwells on death, longing, and loneliness. Smith emphasizes this by contrasting what the speaker says with how she feels. The speaker says she is delighted and calm, but she is neither. Other than those two words, the rest of Smith's word choices are negative—sorrow and suffering, despair and woe.

Smith knew of the moon's power as a symbol. In her sonnet, "Written at the Churchyard at Middleton in Sussex," she calls the moon "mute arbitress of tides." An arbitress is a woman who makes decisions. Smith means that the moon silently has power over the ocean tides. If the moon can move water, it can also, metaphorically, sway emotions.

"To the Moon" follows the rhyme scheme *abab cdcd efef gg*. Its lines are written in iambic pentameter, a meter commonly used in traditional poetry. An iamb is a pair of unstressed and stressed syllables. Pentameter means a meter of five iambs. So each line has five beats. For example, line 2 could be read like this: a-LONE and-PEN sive-I de-LIGHT to-STRAY.

Smith's first lines are descriptive. In line 7, something changes. Traditionally, in the middle of the sonnet, there is a turn, or pivot. The author goes more deeply into the subject matter or changes the poem's topic completely. The lines build to a final idea that often reveals a surprising twist. Often, such conjunctions as *but* or *and* indicate a

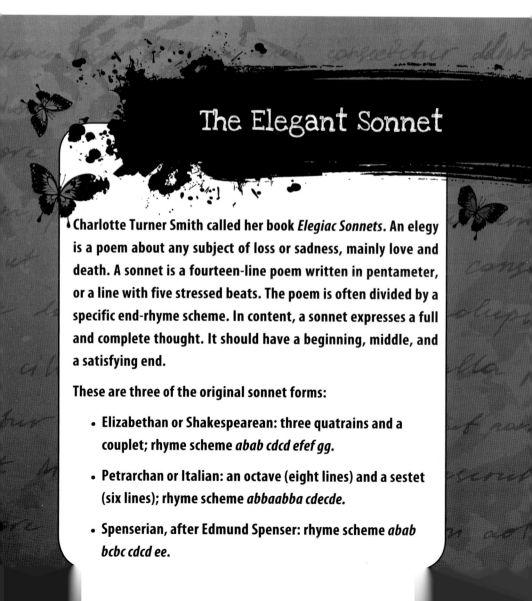

# The Elegant Sonnet

**Charlotte Turner Smith called her book *Elegiac Sonnets*. An elegy is a poem about any subject of loss or sadness, mainly love and death. A sonnet is a fourteen-line poem written in pentameter, or a line with five stressed beats. The poem is often divided by a specific end-rhyme scheme. In content, a sonnet expresses a full and complete thought. It should have a beginning, middle, and a satisfying end.**

**These are three of the original sonnet forms:**

- **Elizabethan or Shakespearean: three quatrains and a couplet; rhyme scheme *abab cdcd efef gg*.**

- **Petrarchan or Italian: an octave (eight lines) and a sestet (six lines); rhyme scheme *abbaabba cdecde*.**

- **Spenserian, after Edmund Spenser: rhyme scheme *abab bcbc cdcd ee*.**

change in direction. They deepen or divide ideas. In "To the Moon," when the speaker says, "And oft I think," she turns away from the moon and into her mind.

In Smith's poetry, critics have noticed that some of her phrases "float." Some phrases are not grammatically clear. In line 2, for example, is it the speaker or the moonbeam that is "alone and pensive"? It is hard to tell.

In the final couplet, some readers might think that by "poor wearied pilgrim," she means the moon. Some critics believe she does this on purpose. In her grammar, she confuses the speaker with the moon to bring them closer. Although the speaker does not feel close to nature, the poet unites them.

Smith's sonnets often build in intensity. In the end, her speakers beg for relief from suffering. They cry out in the last couplet to be released from pain. However, in the end, reality returns, and the speakers are still rooted in misery.

## Thematic Relevance

"To the Moon" is typical of many of Smith's other sonnets. Her speakers often wander alone in a landscape but feel separate from the surroundings. Smith, as one of the earliest Romantic poets, did not describe nature for its beauty alone. She used nature to reflect the human psyche. Her speakers do not name the specific causes of their melancholy.

They are deeply connected to a suffering that is basic to being human.

At the time, in the 1790s, writers were just beginning to view nature as a way to explore the inner self. In an era when women were expected to conceal emotions, Smith wrote frankly about loss and suffering. She knew she was taking a risk by publishing her private words. She was opening herself to public criticism. In the preface to the book's sixth edition, in 1792, she writes: "I am well aware that for a woman—'The post of honour is a private station.'"

Connecting nature's forces to emotions was a new idea. Even though Smith often wrote about nature as an entity incapable of helping her, it was a smart decision to use nature to describe melancholy. Many readers who shared her feelings were able to identify with her poems.

# Further Study Questions

### Recall Questions

1. What elements of the form make a sonnet a challenge to write?

2. How were Charlotte Turner Smith's poems groundbreaking in the time she wrote?

3. What does the speaker claim in the final couplet of "To the Moon"? Briefly summarize her claim.

## Ponder Further

4. Read the sonnet "To the South Downs" below by Charlotte Turner Smith. Explain how the speaker in "To the South Downs" connects her thoughts to nature:

### To the South Downs

*Ah, hills beloved!—where once, a happy child,*
*Your beechen shades, "your turf, your flowers, among,"*
*I wove your bluebells into garlands wild,*
*And woke your echoes with my artless song.*
*Ah! hills beloved!—your turf, your flowers, remain;*
*But can they peace to this sad breast restore,*
*For one poor moment soothe the sense of pain,*
*And teach a broken heart to throb no more?*
*And you, Aruna\*! in the vale\* below,*
*As to the sea your limpid waves you bear,*
*Can you one kind Lethean\* cup bestow,*
*To drink a long oblivion to my care?*
*Ah no!—when all, e'en hope's last ray is gone,*
*There's no oblivion but in death alone!*

---

\***Aruna:** the Arun River in West Sussex, England

\***vale:** valley; also mortal life (as in vale of tears)

\***Lethean:** related to Lethe, a river in Hades, the mythical underworld. Whoever drank the waters of the river Lethe forgot the past.

5. What qualities describe gothic literature? Search
   for a definition of gothic literature. List some of
   the aspects. Is it a genre you think you would like?
   Why or why not? Write a poem of your own with
   gothic elements, one in which a character is alone
   in nature. Try to create a landscape that reflects the
   character's emotions.

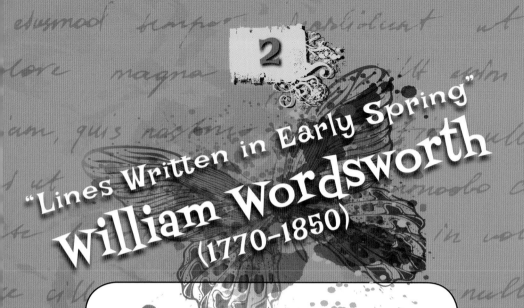

# 2

## "Lines Written in Early Spring"
# William Wordsworth
## (1770–1850)

William Wordsworth revered nature. He often wrote poems in his head during daily walks and felt a unity with nature. He filled his poems with views of mountains, valleys, and lakes. He described nature in grand terms. In his poem, "Lines Composed a Few Miles Above Tintern Abbey," he calls himself "a worshipper of Nature." Wordsworth studied nature's impact on his mind and his emotions, from joy to despair. He connected landscapes to noble themes, such as faith, the soul, mortality, and life's meaning.

Wordsworth preferred simple country life to busy city life. He spent his happiest moments as a child in nature. He grew up in England's Lake District, where he learned to love nature.

William Wordsworth

# Lines Written in Early Spring

I HEARD a thousand blended notes,
While in a grove I sate* reclined,
In that sweet mood when pleasant thoughts
Bring sad thoughts to the mind.

To her fair works did Nature link
The human soul that through me ran;
And much it grieved my heart to think
What man has made of man.

Through primrose tufts, in that green bower*,
The periwinkle trailed its wreaths;
And 'tis my faith that every flower
Enjoys the air it breathes.

The birds around me hopped and played,
Their thoughts I cannot measure:—
But the least motion which they made
It seemed a thrill of pleasure.

The budding twigs spread out their fan,
To catch the breezy air;
And I must think, do all I can,
That there was pleasure there.

If this belief from heaven be sent,
If such be Nature's holy plan,
Have I not reason to lament
What man has made of man?

*sate: sat
*bower: a place to dwell, a shelter; in nature, it might be a
  protected place in a garden.

When he was eight, Wordsworth attended a boarding school. He awoke early to walk and watch the sunrise. He often went horseback riding, ice-skating, and boating. When he was older, he attended St. John's College in Cambridge. During his last year, he went on a walking tour of Europe, walking many miles a day and crossing the Alps mountain range. The natural scenery impressed him deeply.

Wordsworth believed his early experiences in nature opened his imagination. He linked his joy with the rhythms of nature. He carried his childhood memories of nature into his adult life and returned to them repeatedly. He believed a childhood in nature made him a happier adult. In his poem, "The Prelude," he claims his friend and fellow poet Samuel Taylor Coleridge has been "Debarr'd from Nature's living images" because he grew up in a city.

## Summary

Many critics read Wordsworth's poems as autobiographical. His critics and readers consider Wordsworth the speaker of his poems. In "Lines Written in Early Spring," Wordsworth sits alone in a beautiful grove. The setting is simple and serene. He watches the peaceful scene with a sense of melancholy, a mix of sweet, pleasant, and sad feelings. He thinks about what he sees. Something about the natural scene stirs him inside and makes him sad.

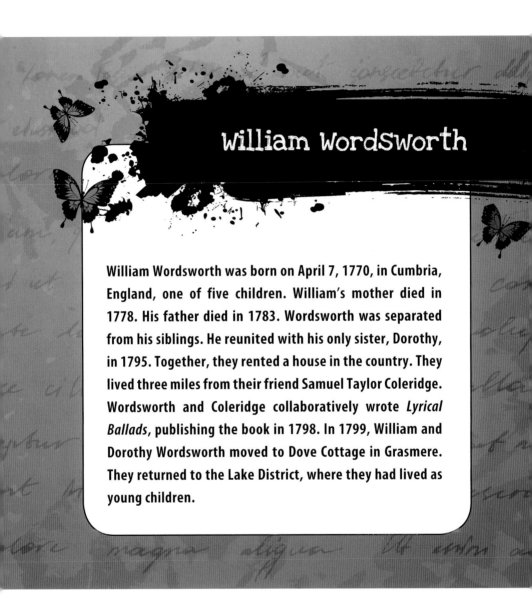

# William Wordsworth

William Wordsworth was born on April 7, 1770, in Cumbria, England, one of five children. William's mother died in 1778. His father died in 1783. Wordsworth was separated from his siblings. He reunited with his only sister, Dorothy, in 1795. Together, they rented a house in the country. They lived three miles from their friend Samuel Taylor Coleridge. Wordsworth and Coleridge collaboratively wrote *Lyrical Ballads*, publishing the book in 1798. In 1799, William and Dorothy Wordsworth moved to Dove Cottage in Grasmere. They returned to the Lake District, where they had lived as young children.

Wordsworth deeply connects with nature in this scene. Nature has linked, he says, "her fair works" to his human soul. He is the only human being present among the plants, animals, and elements. Although he observes nature, his thoughts and his conclusions are about humanity. He describes nature and humanity as separate but intertwined. And as he praises the perfection of nature, he bemoans humanity. He bases his conclusions on his faith and his beliefs.

# Explication

In the poem, written in 1798, Wordsworth states his core belief about nature—that all things living have the ability to feel. He believes that all things, including humans, are more deeply connected to nature than they know. It is also in this poem that Wordsworth establishes his role as a poet. Wordsworth speaks for both nature and humanity. He does not fully identify with either. In the poem, he does not seem to be part of either the scenery or society. In that way, he can be the visionary poet who interprets nature. Note that by "man," he means humanity. Wordsworth wrote in a time when people did not use gender-inclusive or neutral language.

In the opening words of "Lines Written in Early Spring," Wordsworth aligns himself with nature when he states, "I heard a thousand blended notes." The elements of nature have merged. The reader can imagine the "notes" of birds,

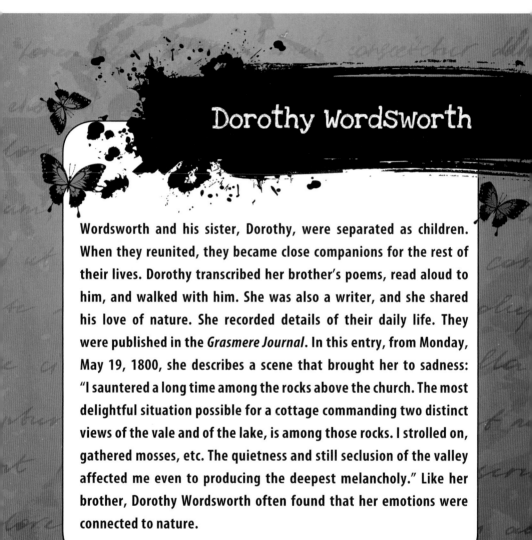

# Dorothy Wordsworth

Wordsworth and his sister, Dorothy, were separated as children. When they reunited, they became close companions for the rest of their lives. Dorothy transcribed her brother's poems, read aloud to him, and walked with him. She was also a writer, and she shared his love of nature. She recorded details of their daily life. They were published in the *Grasmere Journal*. In this entry, from Monday, May 19, 1800, she describes a scene that brought her to sadness: "I sauntered a long time among the rocks above the church. The most delightful situation possible for a cottage commanding two distinct views of the vale and of the lake, is among those rocks. I strolled on, gathered mosses, etc. The quietness and still seclusion of the valley affected me even to producing the deepest melancholy." Like her brother, Dorothy Wordsworth often found that her emotions were connected to nature.

flies, water, and wind, but Wordsworth does not describe those sounds. Wordsworth is the hearer, the witness of nature. He begins to listen to nature, and the reader begins to listen to his thoughts. In that way, Wordsworth speaks for nature.

To open the second stanza, Wordsworth states one of his core beliefs: "To her fair works did Nature link/The human soul that through me ran." He believes human beings are intimately connected to nature. He also believes his role as a poet is to interpret the meaning of nature for readers and, that day, his belief has caused him to grieve. He never describes his own physical experience. Does he sit on a rock, a log, or grass? He admits to neither comfort nor discomfort. His heart and soul are affected by nature, not his body. His physical being does not seem touched. In that way, he does not fully embrace his human self.

In the third, fourth, and fifth stanzas, Wordsworth provides proof for his argument. In the third stanza, he claims that flowers enjoy breathing, like people do. In the fourth stanza, he says birds feel pleasure when they hop around. In the fifth stanza, he makes it sound as if the trees are stretching to enjoy the fresh air.

He has no evidence that flowers, birds, and trees can think and feel, but to him they seem happy and capable of pleasure. He wonders whether his own thought came to him from a divine source. When he says, "If this belief from heaven be sent," he suggests that his human nature comes from earthly nature. He claims to understand "Nature's holy plan."

As Wordsworth sits in a natural setting, he also sits between human beliefs and natural life. He weighs his human faith against the physicality of birds, flowers, and trees. Finally, he says, "Have I not reason to lament/What man has made of man?" He poses it as a question directed to his readers. He sounds critical of humanity, even though he is human. Perhaps he laments, or regrets, that people do not seem to enjoy life as easily as other creatures. At the same time, though, he does not completely accept responsibility for "what man has made of man." He does not even describe what he means by the line. Perhaps he wants to let readers think of their own examples.

# Style, Technique, and Poetic Devices

"Lines Written in Early Spring" has no narrative story. There is no action in the poem. Instead, Wordsworth weaves thoughts about nature and humanity together.

The simplicity of the poem is typical of Wordsworth, who, like other Romantic poets, moves away from the elevated language of earlier poets. He uses the language of everyday conversation. His words are mostly one or two syllables long.

The form of the poem is simple, too. Each of the six four-line stanzas has an *abab* rhyme scheme. The first three lines of each stanza strike a metric four beats. The last line is shortened, marking only three beats.

I **heard** a **thou**sand **blend**ed **notes**,

While **in** a **grove** I **sate** re**clined**,

In **that** sweet **mood** when **pleas**ant **thoughts**

Bring **sad** thoughts **to** the **mind**.

He repeats one line twice: "What man has made of man." It is an important line. Notice that the word *man* is stressed both times it is spoken.

Using the device of personification, Wordsworth links nature and humanity. He gives nature human qualities. His flowers breathe. Birds are happy. Trees feel the breeze. He refers to nature as female, even though nature does not have a specific gender identity. Wordsworth also gives human beings qualities of nature. Nature operates by instinct. Wordsworth wonders whether his own beliefs are instinctive. He wonders whether they come from some place other than his own reason.

# Thematic Relevance

Wordsworth has been praised as an interpreter of nature. He interprets the meaning of nature's works in a way no other author does. He wrote many of his poems outdoors. He would sit and observe a place until it influenced his thoughts. Forty years after writing "Lines Written in Early Spring," he could still recall the scene that inspired it. He writes that the poem was "actually composed while I was sitting beside the brook that runs down from the Comb, in which stands the village of Alford. . . ."

Some scholars believe that such poems as "Lines Written in Early Spring" reflect a growing maturity that leads to his longer poems, such as "Tintern Abbey." In 1802, Wordsworth married Mary Hutchison. A few months after he died, on April 23, 1850, his wife, Mary, published his long poem titled "The Prelude." The long poem is considered one of his most important achievements. Readers and critics praised the poet for being so in tune with nature. Wordsworth could interpret and understand nature in a way no other author could.

Based on his childhood, Wordsworth believed that all children need to play in nature. His views influenced education. Prior to his Romantic thinking, children were simply moved into adulthood as fast as possible. Wordsworth helped educators view school as a place to nurture children.

His work also influenced ideas about conservation. He inspired the National Trust to protect England's land. Wordsworth was and still is considered one of the most important nature poets. In *The Spirit of the Age: Contemporary Portraits*, published in 1825, William Hazlitt wrote that Wordsworth "calms the throbbing pulses of his own heart, by keeping his eye ever fixed on the face of nature."

# Further Study Questions

**Recall Questions**

1. What is the poem's main idea in "Lines Written in Early Spring"?

2. What was one of Wordsworth's purposes in writing nature poetry?

3. Where are the stressed beats in the last line of the sixth stanza, "What man has made of man"?

**Ponder Further**

4. Refer to John Clare's poem in Chapter 4, "The Mouse's Nest." Compare Wordsworth's speaker to John Clare's speaker. How are the two speakers alike or different? What other comparisons can you make between the two speakers?

5. Ralph Waldo Emerson (1803–1882) is sometimes called an American Wordsworth. As a child, Emerson read Wordsworth's poems. Read a short nature poem by Emerson, such as "Water," "April," or "Berrying." What ideas about nature does Emerson seem to share with Wordsworth?

# 3

## "Frost at Midnight"
## Samuel Taylor Coleridge
### (1772–1834)

Samuel Taylor Coleridge loved to daydream. It fueled his creativity. His poems are filled with his imaginative visions. "Mild splendour of the various-vested Night!/Mother of wildly-working visions!" he writes in his sonnet "To the Autumnal Moon." In those lines, he praises the source of his imagination: nature.

In 1794, Coleridge met Robert Southey, and in 1795, he befriended William Wordsworth. The three were called the Lake Poets because they lived in England's Lake District, a region famous for its lakes, forests, and mountains (and now a National Park). Wordsworth grew up in the Lake District. Coleridge, though, was raised in London. He felt cheated of the joyful childhood in nature that Wordsworth enjoyed. It did not prevent him from appreciating the outdoors. He dreamed of a world in which humans, animals, and nature all lived in harmony. Wordsworth, in his "Poem for Coleridge," calls Coleridge "[t]he most intense of Nature's worshippers."

Coleridge and Wordsworth took many walks together. Besides discussing philosophy, religion, and politics, they talked about new ways to write poetry. They decided to use simple diction, new meters, and natural themes. They wanted to borrow the form of the ballad, a poem that includes elements of songs and folktales. In some of those stories, they planned to infuse nature with the supernatural. They also wanted their poems to use traditional poetic devices.

The two poets collaborated on a book called *Lyrical Ballads,* first published in 1798. The book helped launch literature's Romantic era. Coleridge's main contribution was his long poem "Rime of the Ancient Mariner." During the next five or six years, he wrote some of his best poems, such as "Kubla Khan," "Fears in Solitude," "Christabel," and "Frost at Midnight."

Despite his intense poetic imagination, Coleridge had trouble completing and publishing his works. Whole poems often came to him as intense, full visions. He had trouble capturing them in words on paper. For much of his life, he struggled with insecurity.

# Frost at Midnight

The Frost performs its secret ministry,
Unhelped by any wind. The owlet's cry
Came loud—and hark, again! loud as before.
The inmates of my cottage, all at rest,
Have left me to that solitude, which suits
Abstruser* musings: save that at my side
My cradled infant slumbers peacefully.
'Tis calm indeed! so calm, that it disturbs
And vexes* meditation with its strange
And extreme silentness. Sea, hill, and wood,
This populous village! Sea, and hill, and wood,
With all the numberless goings-on of life,
Inaudible as dreams! the thin blue flame
Lies on my low-burnt fire, and quivers not;
Only that film, which fluttered on the grate,

Still flutters there, the sole unquiet thing.
Methinks, its motion in this hush of nature
Gives it dim sympathies with me who live,
Making it a companionable form,
Whose puny flaps and freaks the idling Spirit
By its own moods interprets, every where
Echo or mirror seeking of itself,
And makes a toy of Thought.

But O! how oft*,
How oft, at school, with most believing mind,
Presageful*, have I gazed upon the bars,
To watch that fluttering stranger! and as oft
With unclosed lids, already had I dreamt
Of my sweet birth-place, and the old church-tower,
Whose bells, the poor man's only music, rang
From morn to evening, all the hot Fair-day,
So sweetly, that they stirred and haunted me
With a wild pleasure, falling on mine ear
Most like articulate sounds of things to come!
So gazed I, till the soothing things, I dreamt,
Lulled me to sleep, and sleep prolonged my dreams!
And so I brooded all the following morn,
Awed by the stern preceptor's face, mine eye
Fixed with mock study on my swimming book:
Save if the door half opened, and I snatched
A hasty glance, and still my heart leaped up,
For still I hoped to see the stranger's face,
Townsman, or aunt, or sister more beloved,
My play-mate when we both were clothed alike!

Dear Babe, that sleepest cradled by my side,
Whose gentle breathings, heard in this deep calm,
Fill up the interspersèd vacancies
And momentary pauses of the thought!
My babe so beautiful! it thrills my heart
With tender gladness, thus to look at thee,
And think that thou shalt learn far other lore,

And in far other scenes! For I was reared
In the great city, pent 'mid cloisters dim,
And saw nought lovely but the sky and stars.
But thou, my babe! shalt wander like a breeze
By lakes and sandy shores, beneath the crags
Of ancient mountain, and beneath the clouds,
Which image in their bulk both lakes and shores
And mountain crags: so shalt thou see and hear
The lovely shapes and sounds intelligible
Of that eternal language, which thy God
Utters, who from eternity doth teach
Himself in all, and all things in himself.
Great universal Teacher! he shall mould
Thy spirit, and by giving make it ask.

    Therefore all seasons shall be sweet to thee,
Whether the summer clothe the general earth
With greenness, or the redbreast sit and sing
Betwixt the tufts of snow on the bare branch
Of mossy apple-tree, while the nigh thatch
Smokes in the sun-thaw; whether the eave-drops fall
Heard only in the trances of the blast,
Or if the secret ministry of frost
Shall hang them up in silent icicles,
Quietly shining to the quiet Moon.

***Abstruser:** more difficult to understand

***vexes:** irritates

***oft:** short for *often*

***Presageful:** able to predict; to have knowledge that something
   will happen

# Samuel Taylor Coleridge

Samuel Taylor Coleridge, born on October 21, 1772, in Devonshire, England, was the youngest of fourteen children. When Coleridge was nine, his father died. The boy was sent to a boarding school. He was often punished for daydreaming, which later gave him nightmares. In 1791, he began to study religion at Cambridge. He was a brilliant student, both intelligent and creative. Although he lacked the patience to complete a degree, he became a well-regarded journalist, Shakespeare scholar, and poetry critic.

He married Sarah Fricker, and the couple had four children. Illnesses that Coleridge suffered as a child followed him into adulthood. For the rest of his life, he suffered from anxiety and depression. To treat his illnesses, Coleridge became addicted to opium, a substance prescribed as pain medicine. It is not known whether his drug addiction fueled or suppressed his creativity, or how much it led to his fears, anxiety, depression, and other illnesses. He died of a heart attack on July 25, 1834, at the age of sixty-one.

# Summary

"Frost at Midnight" takes place in a cottage in a small village at night in winter. In a cozy room, Coleridge sits beside a fireplace with his baby, fast asleep in a cradle. Everyone else in the house is asleep.

The outside world is quiet. The house is so calm that he feels unsettled. The only movement is from the fireplace. He is glad that there is another restless spirit in the house besides himself. However, the film flickering on the flames makes "a toy of Thought." Watching the fire puts him into a trance of sorts. It stirs his memories.

Now deep in thought, he recalls being in school. He was acutely aware of the presence of a stranger outside the classroom. He tried to see this person—it may have been someone ringing a church bell. The music seemed to chime out "things to come!" The childhood incident is meaningful but also a little frustrating. In his memory, he never sees the person.

Instead, his baby stirs in the cradle. His child returns him to the present moment. He makes a promise to his child when he says, "[T]hou . . . shalt wander like a breeze/ By lakes and sandy shores, beneath the crags/Of ancient mountain, and beneath the clouds. . . ." His child will enjoy the freedoms of nature that he missed in his own childhood.

# Explication

In "Frost at Midnight," Coleridge's use of his conversational style allows him to transform a negative memory into hope for his baby's childhood. First, the quiet night changes his restless mood to one of peace. In a calm state, he can think through a problem. The poem seems to happen in real time in the present moment. Sitting beside the fire is not a remembered past event. In this conversational poem, Coleridge makes it seem as if he has recorded his wandering thoughts as they come to him.

Time is important in the poem. As he meditates, Coleridge travels into the past and looks toward the future. From the title "Frost at Midnight," he establishes that it is winter and midnight, the "zero hour." In the present moment, the outside world seems far away, "inaudible as dreams." In this unmoving scene, his restless thoughts keep changing. The poem's action is internal, not external. The "hush of nature" pushes his thoughts to wander.

When flames flutter in the fireplace grate, Coleridge thinks the fire is as restless as he is. That is when something otherworldly happens. An "idling Spirit" overtakes Coleridge. This mystical phenomena or sensation "makes a toy of Thought." He is subject to the whims of his imagination. In those eight lines, Coleridge transitions away from the present moment beside the fire, and, in a sleepy trance, he remembers a past experience.

When he recalls dreaming and practically falling asleep in school, he merges his childhood self with his adult self. As an adult before the fire or a schoolchild looking out a window, he is lost in the world of his imagination. Recalling the past, he finds the "[e]cho or mirror seeking of itself." As a boy, he was fascinated by a stranger, someone who probably rang the church bells. When he could not see this person, he failed to understand and learn. The experience frustrated him terribly. His childhood lacked something. He attributes his failure, in part, to the absence of nature in his childhood. He never sees the stranger in his memory. Just as one restless spirit drew him into his meditation, another draws him out. He hears his child breathing in the cradle, and he snaps out of his trance.

Coleridge is then struck by an insight. His childhood is over. He can't change it. His baby's childhood has not begun, however. He vows to raise his son in the beauty of nature, not the noise of a city. In any season, his child will be educated by the "Great universal Teacher," not a "stern preceptor." His final image includes the "ministry of the frost." He brings himself, and the reader, back to where he started, in a cabin in winter. When Coleridge returns, full circle, to the fireplace, his thoughts have changed. Because he suffered as a child in a city, he will make sure his child is happy in nature.

# Style, Technique, and Poetic Devices

"Frost at Midnight" is one of Coleridge's "conversation poems." He starts the poem in a problematic state. He ponders a question. He rambles a bit. As he talks through his question, he reaches an answer. He has an insight. He solves his problem. He seems to speak to himself. In that way, the poem's readers become eavesdroppers, listening in on his intimate thoughts.

The poem, written in the present tense, begins in a warm, tender scene. When an owl hoots, Coleridge cries "Hark!" as if hearing it in that instant, not from memory. The scene happens in real time, as if he writes his thoughts as they occur to him. The rhythm of the poem is gentle and lulling. The language is close to natural speech. Although written in iambic pentameter, the stress patterns are soft and barely noticeable.

Coleridge's main device is symbolism. His images represent a deeper meaning. For example, the owl, full moon, and fire can be seen as symbols of wisdom. He repeats images and words to emphasize a greater significance. When he uses the word "fluttering" to refer to both the fire and a school memory, he makes the fire a symbol of his childhood. He reinforces his connection to his past.

Frost is also symbolic. The frost on the window may represent the death of his childhood and his separation from the outer world. However, the frost also does work for nature. In the first line, when frost "performs its secret ministry," frost is personified. It is not just ice but an entity that can serve humanity and nature in a very valuable, meaningful way.

In the end, Coleridge returns to the "secret ministry of frost." The poem comes full circle. He ends the poem by looking up at the moon. The sky was the only image of nature he had as a child. The distant moon reinforces Coleridge's lost connection with the earth.

# Thematic Relevance

In "Frost at Midnight," Coleridge mourns the loss of nature in his own childhood but joyfully anticipates experiences of nature for his children. "Frost at Midnight" is an intimate poem. Coleridge wrote it during a happy time in his life. He and his wife, Sarah Fricker, had just had their baby son, Hartley. On a cold February night in 1798, Coleridge had this experience as he watched the child. In September of that year, he sold the poem with two others, titling the group of poems *Fears in Solitude*.

"Frost at Midnight" illustrates Coleridge's creative habit of sinking deep into his imagination before writing, and it shows a Romantic interpretation of nature. Romantics believed nature plays a role in a child's development. Romantics believed that children learn their connection to nature. Adults lose the feeling of unity with nature and must depend on their childhood memories. Coleridge mourned his childhood in London. He believed his growth was flawed. (Poets Charles Lamb and Lord Byron, on the other hand, did not accept these beliefs about nature.)

Still, like Wordsworth, who believed that memory feeds poetic imagination, Coleridge allowed his memory to spark a larger poem. In his *Biographia Literaria*, published in 1817, Coleridge wrote that in spite of his flaws and weaknesses, "there was a long and blessed interval, during which my natural faculties were allowed to expand, and my original tendencies to develop themselves;—my fancy, and the love of nature, and the sense of beauty in forms and sounds."

# Further Study Questions

**Recall Questions**

1. Where, when, and with whom is Coleridge sitting in the poem?

2. What makes "Frost at Midnight" a conversational poem?

3. Briefly summarize Coleridge's childhood memory, in lines 24 to 42. Why do you think this memory was so significant to him?

### Ponder Further

4. Compare "Frost at Midnight" to "Lines Written in Early Spring" by William Wordsworth. Make a two-column chart and jot notes. Point out simple differences and similarities. At the bottom of your chart, write a few sentences comparing the poems.

| "Lines Written in Early Spring" | "Frost at Midnight" |
|---|---|
| Short | Long |
| sits outside in nature | sits inside a cottage |
|  |  |
|  |  |
|  |  |
|  |  |
|  |  |
| Comparison Comments: | |

5. How do nature's seasons shape a poem? Online or in the library, find another winter poem, such as "Winter-Time" by Robert Louis Stevenson, "The Snow-Storm" by Ralph Waldo Emerson, "Stopping by Woods on a Snowy Evening" by Robert Frost, or "The Snow Man" by Wallace Stevens. What aspects of winter shape a poem's theme and tone?

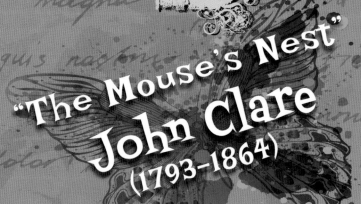

# "The Mouse's Nest"
## John Clare
### (1793–1864)

John Clare was born on July 18, 1793, in Helpston, England, the hometown of his parents, Parker and Ann. Raised in poverty, John worked to pay for his own schooling, where he learned to read. At age thirteen, he read his first book of poems, *The Seasons* by Scottish poet James Thomson (1700–1748). On his way to town to buy a copy of the book, he composed, in his head, his first poem, "The Morning Walk." Some of his poems did not survive. He used the paper he wrote them on to light the daily fire.

Often called a peasant poet, Clare lived most of his life where he was born, in Helpston, a Northamptonshire village in England. He did not travel. Instead, he observed the natural world close to home. Instead of sweeping views of mountains, he looked at bugs in the grass right at his feet. Clare was a self-taught botanist who discovered many species. As a poet, he brought awareness to the ordinary, familiar world around him. As he wrote in his sonnet "Swordy Well," Clare saw "the wonders of great nature's plan/In trifles insignificant and small."

Once asked where he got ideas for his poems, Clare claimed he kicked them out of the "clods," or lumps of dirt. He composed poems in the fields as he worked. Clare's first book sold well. Published in 1820, *Poems Descriptive of Rural Life and Scenery* made Clare a popular nature poet. This humble farmer turned poet fascinated readers. At first, Clare earned money. His fame and fortune did not last, however.

Romantic poets, such as William Wordsworth, expressed sublime joy or deep melancholy. Clare, however, did not infuse his nature poems with intense emotions. Rather than record a speaker's inner experience of nature, he looked outward and described what he saw. In this way, Clare inspired emotional responses in his readers.

John Keats complained about Clare's descriptive poems, saying that "description too much prevailed over sentiment." Keats wanted more emotion. Clare responded that Keats "described nature as she appeared to his fancys and not as he would have described had he witnessed the things he describes." For Clare, Keats was too interested in his imagination.

# John Clare

For forty years, Clare lived in the family cottage where he was born. He and his wife, Patty, had seven children. Clare struggled to earn a living as a farm laborer. In 1832, a few years before Clare published "The Mouse's Nest," a friend wanted to help Clare. He offered Clare and his family the use of a larger cottage on some land in Northborough, only three miles away.

John Clare delayed the move, to his wife's frustration and his friend's puzzlement. He did not want to leave his childhood home. Finally, Patty packed up and began the short walk to their new home. Clare trudged behind, allegedly, with his eyes almost closed, as if he were in pain or having a bad dream.

Five years later, in 1837, he was committed to an insane asylum. He escaped and walked eighty miles in four days to return home. He was placed in the Northampton asylum, closer to his home. He lived there for twenty-three years until his death in 1864.

John Clare

# The Mouse's Nest

I found a ball of grass among the hay
And proged* it as I passed and went away;
And when I looked I fancied something stirred,
And turned again and hoped to catch the bird—
When out an old mouse bolted in the wheats
With all her young ones hanging at her teats;
She looked so odd and so grotesque to me,
I ran and wondered what the thing could be,
And pushed the knapweed bunches where I stood;
Then the mouse hurried from the craking* brood.
The young ones squeaked, and as I went away
She found her nest again among the hay.
The water o'er the pebbles scarce could run
And broad old cesspools glittered in the sun.

*proged: kicked

*craking: crying harshly

For the most part, Clare's poems do not include moral directives, arguments, or conclusions. Even so, Clare was concerned with the human encroachment on nature. In his 1809 poem "Helpstone," he wrote:

> How oft I've sigh'd at alterations made,
> To see the woodman's cruel axe employ'd
> A tree beheaded, or bush destroy'd.

Many of Clare's poems describe human interactions with nature. In "The Mouse's Nest," the speaker has a comical encounter with an animal.

## Summary

"The Mouse's Nest," published in 1835, tells a story of a man walking along, kicking at the ground. The speaker carelessly tromps through a field. He accidentally kicks a clod. Seeing movement, he tries to catch a bird. The nest he has disturbed, to his surprise, belongs to a mouse.

The mouse nurses her brood. Surprised herself, she breaks away from her pups. Man and mouse part ways, knowing as little about each other as when they met. The speaker continues on his way, claiming the mouse returned to her nest. Whether she truly did or not is unknown.

## Explication

In "The Mouse's Nest," just as the speaker exposes a nest, Clare exposes a human tendency to destroy nature.

From the start, the speaker is thoughtless and destructive. When he stumbles on a nest, he hopes to catch, and thereby harm, a bird. This is a clue that he has destructive impulses. Instead, a mouse startles him. It's not her fault. The field is the natural home of creatures such as mice. He is the intruder, not she. She was trying to stay hidden. The man exposes her, disturbing her private act of feeding her pups and her desperate act of survival, raising her species.

Unlike the autobiographical speakers in Wordsworth's poems, who are serene in nature, Clare's speakers are often puzzled by nature in a way Clare was not. Instead of feeling compassion for the mouse or remorse for his actions, the speaker focuses on his response. To him, the mouse looks odd and grotesque. It is as if her sight repulses him. He lacks awareness of what has happened. After seeing the mouse, in line 5, he still "wondered what the thing could be," in line 8. Confronted with a truth about nature, he cannot take it in.

The speaker states only one detail about the mouse: she has "all her young ones hanging at her teats." He does not explain why he finds her "odd" and "grotesque," but in calling her so, Clare suggests that the fault lies in the speaker's human misperception, not the mouse's presence.

Unlike Clare himself—who would have relished watching the mouse—the speaker rushes off, not knowing how much damage he has done. But the mouse hurries from her brood. Her link with her pups may be broken. In line 12, the speaker claims the mouse found her nest again, but how can he know? He doesn't watch to find out. The mouse's story is not concluded.

In the poem's last two lines, the speaker looks up at the larger world. He sees water, pebbles, cesspools, and sun. They seem like random sights: "The water o'er the pebbles scarce could run./And broad old cesspools glittered in the sun." A river is dry. The natural source of water, or life, struggles. However, a septic sewage well shines. A man-made water container appears beautiful. In light of the mouse's tragedy, these images represent the clash between nature and humans.

The final word in the poem, *sun,* is as far from a mouse's nest as nature can get. The speaker looks up from the mouse's nest. Is he changed? Does he even remember the incident? At the same time, readers, looking up from the poem, might be asking themselves the same questions!

# Style, Technique, and Poetic Devices

Critics call "The Mouse's Nest" masterful because of its structure. Although written in past tense, the action happens quickly. By surprising his hapless speaker, Clare seems to want to surprise the reader, too. Small creatures such as snakes or insects tend to frighten people. Throughout the poem, Clare seems to test the reader's response.

Clare loved ballads, stories, and folktales. Doesn't the story in "The Mouse's Nest" seem like a fable? Notice that the speaker commits eleven actions—he progs, finds, passes, looks, turns, hopes, runs, wonders, pushes, stands, and goes away. All these active verbs heighten the speaker's agitation in the field and his dominance in the poem. The mouse only gets three active verbs—she bolts, hurries, and finds. This unequal balance shows that the man overbears the mouse.

In form, the poem is a sonnet, fourteen rhyming lines written in iambic pentameter. Each ten-syllable line has five "feet," rhythmic units of one unstressed and one stressed syllable. The rhythm of the lines sounds like this: daDUM daDUM daDUM daDUM daDUM.

˘ / ˘ / ˘ / ˘ / ˘ /
I **found** a **ball** of **grass** a**mong** the **hay**

˘ / ˘ / ˘ / ˘ / ˘ /
And **proged** it **as** I **passed** and **went** a**way**;

Clare wrote many poems about nests, and many are sonnets. A traditional English, or Shakespearean, sonnet is divided into three quatrains and a final couplet. The first quatrain introduces a topic. The second develops a conflict. The third suggests a new way to view it. The final couplet concludes the argument.

Applying this structure to "The Mouse's Nest," in the first quatrain, the man disrupts nature. In the second, mouse and man face each other. In the third, the man leaves the mouse to suffer the consequences.

In "The Mouse's Nest," Clare does not use a traditional rhyme scheme of alternating lines. Instead, he rhymes pairs of lines, or couplets: *aa bb/cc dd/ee aa/ff*. Notice that lines 1 and 2 and 11 and 12 repeat the *a*-rhyme words *hay* and *away*. In this way, Clare makes the brief encounter between mouse and man more significant. He gives the form a circular closure but not the story.

The final couplet, in a dramatic turn, contains neither mouse nor man. The lines describe a new scene that juxtaposes man-made and natural images. Clare purposefully allows his storyline to fall apart, but he controls the sonnet to hold the poem together. In resolving the poem's form, he asks readers to participate more fully in its puzzling content.

# Thematic Relevance

Clare did not live in a dramatic landscape. There were no oceans or mountain views. He lived on simple flat farmland. This might be why Clare grew fascinated with the small, hidden aspects of nature right at his feet.

Unlike the speaker in "The Mouse's Nest," Clare was acutely aware of his surroundings. He loved nests. He searched for these hidden spots that animals try to guard

# What Did John Clare Look Like?

In 1908, poet, critic, and translator Arthur Symons wrote an introduction to a volume of poems by John Clare. Symons described Clare's physical and emotional state:

*Clare is said to have been barely five feet in height, "with keen, eager eyes, high forehead, long hair, falling down in wild and almost grotesque fashion over his shoulders." He was generally dressed in very poor clothes, and was said by some woman to look "like a nobleman in disguise." His nerves were not the nerves of a peasant. Everything that touched him was a delight or an agony, and we hear continually of his bursting into tears. He was restless and loved wandering, but he came back always to the point from which he had started. He could not endure that anything he had once known should be changed. . . . His last words, when he died in the madhouse, were, "I want to go home."*

from humans. He stood and peered into them. In "The Thrush's Nest," although the speaker refers to himself as an "intruding guest," he creeps close enough to see the bird's "shining eggs, as bright as flowers." His nest poems are often about birds—"Quail's Nest," "The Nightingale's Nest," and "The Yellowhammer's Nest," to name a few. Nests were symbolic for Clare. In "Approaching Night," the speaker finishes a workday and says, "Like bird that finds its nest/I'll stop and take my rest."

Nests represent what Clare loved most: the safe intimacy of home. His poems have a stark, raw quality in part because he does not glamorize or idealize nature. He often does not interpret his images. He leaves readers to do that work. Leaving the mouse story incomplete ensures that readers will continue to think about it.

# Further Study Questions

**Recall Questions**

1. Where is the mouse's nest located? Why is the location of the nest important to the poem?

2. How does Clare contrast the poem's content with its form?

3. What does the speaker assume about the mouse?

**Ponder Further**

4. How do you envision the speaker? What kind of person is he? Do you think the speaker changes? Provide details from the poem to support your claim.

5. Clare's poem does not have a clear ending. The last two lines leave the poem open to interpretation. How would you end the story in the poem? Challenge yourself! Put your thoughts into poetry. Write one more couplet to conclude the poem.

# 5

## "A Sea-Side Walk"
## Elizabeth Barrett Browning
## (1806-1861)

In 1832, Elizabeth Barrett Browning's father sold the family estate, and the Barretts moved to a cottage in Sidmouth, a town in Devonshire, England. Sidmouth was quaint enough, and the cottage had an ocean view. In a letter to a friend, Mrs. James Martin, in September 1832, Barrett wrote: "I always thought that the sea was the sublimest object in nature." She never tired of looking at the ocean, with its tempests and motion, storms and calm.

After three years, when the family moved to London, Barrett missed the ocean. On January 1, 1836, she wrote again to Mrs. Martin: "Half my soul, in the meantime, seems to have stayed behind on the seashore." In 1838, she published

Elizabeth Barrett Browning

# A Sea-Side Walk

We walked beside the sea,
After a day which perished silently
Of its own glory—like the Princess weird
Who, combating the Genius, scorched and seared,
Uttered with burning breath, "Ho! victory!"
And sank adown, an heap of ashes pale;
So runs the Arab tale*.

The sky above us showed
A universal and unmoving cloud,
On which, the cliffs permitted us to see
Only the outline of their majesty,
As master-minds, when gazed at by the crowd!
And, shining with a gloom, the water grey
Swang in its moon-taught way.

Nor moon nor stars were out.
They did not dare to tread so soon about,
Though trembling, in the footsteps of the sun.
The light was neither night's nor day's, but one
Which, life-like, had a beauty in its doubt;
And Silence's impassioned breathings round
Seemed wandering into sound.

O solemn-beating heart
Of nature! I have knowledge that thou art
Bound unto man's by cords he cannot sever—
And, what time they are slackened by him ever,
So to attest his own supernal* part,
Still runneth thy vibration fast and strong,
The slackened cord along.

For though we never spoke
Of the grey water and the shaded rock,—
Dark wave and stone, unconsciously, were fused
Into the plaintive* speaking that we used,
Of absent friends and memories unforsook*;
And, had we seen each other's face, we had
Seen haply*, each was sad.

*Arab tale: a literary reference to the book *One Thousand and One Nights,* also called *Arabian Nights,* a collection of Middle Eastern folktales that date back to as early as the ninth century.

*supernal: lofty; coming from above; heavenly or divine

*plaintive: sorrowful

*unforsook: not forgotten

*haply: perhaps

*The Seraphim, and Other Poems*, which included the poem "A Sea-Side Walk." Her health suffered in London. Her doctors encouraged her to visit a warmer climate. She went to the coast town Torquay with Edward, the favorite of her eight brothers. The trip turned into the worst tragedy of her life. The sea became her enemy. While sailing on July 11, 1840, Edward and two of his friends drowned.

Barrett collapsed, physically and emotionally. She was too weak to leave the now-hated Torquay. Friends feared she was close to death. The sound of the sea became a horror to her. Finally, a year later, she returned to London. She shut herself in her dark bedroom, becoming a recluse. She engaged again in reading and writing poetry, but she refused to speak of the tragedy.

# Summary

In the poem, some people walk beside the ocean at dusk. The sun has already set. The poem's first word, the pronoun "we," is never clarified. It might be a pair or a group of companions. The speaker does not specify whom she walks with in the poem.

Nature, not humanity, is active in the poem. The sky shows its clouds. The cliffs only allow part of themselves to be seen. The planets seem to walk across the sky. Surrounded by nature, the speaker has a revelation. She realizes how deeply connected people are to nature.

In the end, she returns to her conversation with her walking companions. In contrast to her amazing insight, they talk about sad things, such as absent friends and past memories.

# Explication

In "A Sea-Side Walk," people stroll on a seashore but are not conscious of the hold nature has over them. The speaker describes the sea, sky, and cliffs, but her companion speaks about "absent friends and memories unforsook." The speaker sees nature, but her friend does not. In that way, the poem's topic is about how people respond to nature. Barrett Browning's point is that people are unaware of their connection to nature even as they stand in its glory. This poem has been called "Wordsworthian" because it shares one of Wordsworth's main themes that humans are linked with nature—emotionally and physically—more than some people can recognize.

Because their awareness of nature is narrow, it makes sense that the poem takes place in nature's borders. The two people walk between the land and the ocean. They stand between sky and earth, and they exist in time's border as well, between day and night. The sun has set, and the moon is about to rise. These boundaries of land and time are narrow, and so is the space the people take up. The people play a small role in the poem. In this narrow space, the people are able to enter the world of nature if they want to, if they let themselves.

# Elizabeth Barrett Browning

Born March 6, 1806, in Durham, England, Elizabeth Barrett Browning was the oldest of eleven children. Although her father was wealthy, she lived in a time when daughters were not allowed an education. She joined her brothers' tutored lessons, and she taught herself. By the age of twelve, she read classics, wrote poems, and studied languages. At age fifteen, perhaps from a spinal injury, she suffered the first of many illnesses. She was twenty-two when her mother died. She lived under her father's loving but stern care. Frail and in poor health, she had anxiety and weak lungs. For some reason, her father forbade his daughter to marry. She stayed in her room and did little but read and write.

Then, in 1844, Elizabeth Barrett published a volume called *Poems*. In one poem, she praised the poet Robert Browning. He wrote to her in January 1845: "I love your verses with all my heart, dear Miss Barrett." From the beginning, they felt connected as poets. They began to write letters back and forth. In May 1845, Browning visited her. They had already fallen in love through their letters. Now they fell in love in person. In the year of their courtship, they wrote a combined 573 love letters. In September 1846, the couple secretly married. Her disapproving father disowned her. Barrett Browning never spoke to him again.

She began a new life. She moved with her husband to Florence, Italy. Her life was happy, and she was in love. The warm climate improved her health. In 1849, the couple had a son. They named him Robert Weidemann Barrett Browning but called him Pen. In 1850, Barrett Browning published *Sonnets From the Portuguese*, love poems written to her husband. They are considered the greatest love poems written in the English language. One of her most famous begins with the line, "How do I love thee? Let me count the ways." She lived in Italy for the rest of her life. She died in her husband's arms on June 29, 1861.

The speaker has been acutely aware of nature, and, at the heart of the poem, she merges with nature. In the fourth stanza, she proclaims, "O solemn-beating heart/of nature! I have knowledge. . . ." It is the only time she uses the singular pronoun "I." She has a private epiphany, experiencing the deep connection between herself and nature. She says that nature's heart is connected to humanity's with a cord that cannot be severed. She also implies that the cord is only ever slack on the human side.

To prove this point, she herself returns to ignoring nature. She rejoins human society. Immediately after her revelation, the speaker returns to the conversation with her friend. Nature is absent in their conversation. Absence is a theme in other ways in this nature poem. Nature reflects the theme of absence. The sun has set, but the moon and stars are not yet in the sky. The cliffs are shaded, and only their outline can be seen.

The speaker sees something that many people miss out on through lack of awareness. Her friend does not know how significantly the landscape has influenced their conversation. The speaker implies that humans feel separate from each other as well as from nature. They talk about absent friends and past memories they can't let go of. They do not talk about the landscape. They can't even see each other's expressions.

# Style, Technique, and Poetic Devices

"A Sea-Side Walk" would be mournful if not for its bright tone. Barrett Browning describes "grey water" as "shining with a gloom" and swinging "in its moon-taught way." Those bright phrases are exciting, not somber. Unlike Charlotte Turner Smith's speaker, who mournfully claims to be happy, Barrett Browning's speaker cheerfully claims to be sad. Each speaker's tone is opposite of what she says.

There is a tremendous sense of adventure in the poem's language. In part, the liveliness is due to the personification of nature. To say in lines 2 and 3 that the day "perished silently/Of its own glory" makes it sound as if the sun is a swashbuckler. The cliffs permit others to see them or not. The moon, stars, and sun can walk. Personification may also be a projection of the speaker's own intimate relationship with nature. And the words further signify that nature is not only trying to interact with the people on the beach, but it has in fact altered their view of nature.

In the first stanza, she interrupts the sea-side walk to summarize a story about the "Princess Weird." The literary reference is from "The Story of the Envious Man," a tale from the *Arabian Nights*. In one way, the poem contains a story within a story. The human action is a walk on a beach. But the speaker does not focus on that part. The real story happens in her imaginative vision of nature.

# Thematic Relevance

"A Sea-Side Walk" was included in the 1838 book *The Seraphim, and Other Poems*. Barrett Browning is known for her imaginative use of language. She loved to pack fantastic imagery into her lines of verse. Her figurative language was called dazzling and glittering.

At least one critic called "A Sea-Side Walk" Barrett Browning's best nature poem. She studied the classics. Some of her main themes are love and loss, and religious devotion and doubt. She also had a strong social conscience and spoke out against slavery, child labor, and the suppression of women.

She often included nature imagery in her poems, however. Some descriptions are happy memories of her childhood estate home, Hope End. The natural settings inspired her imagination. In "The Deserted Garden," she recalls going alone to a forgotten, neglected garden: "I call'd the place my wilderness/For no one enter'd there but I." In the poem, she sits under a tree and dreams of people long dead who may have loved the garden in the past. These morbid thoughts only seem to delight her more:

> *It did not move my grief to see*
> *The trace of human step departed:*
> *Because the garden was deserted,*
> > *The blither place for me!*

# Further Study Questions

### Recall Questions

1. How does Barrett Browning personify nature? Use a phrase from the poem as an example.

2. What does the speaker hear just before she exclaims, "O solemn-beating heart of nature?"

3. Examine the rhyme and meter in each stanza. What rhyme scheme does she use? What metric pattern does she use?

### Ponder Further

4. The speaker walks along the shore at dusk. Why are the setting and time important to this poem? What impact do they have on the poem's message and on the reading experience?

5. In the library or online, find a copy of *Sonnets From the Portuguese*. Search through the forty-four sonnets. Find one that uses nature imagery, such as "Sonnet XXI" or "Sonnet XXXII." How does she describe nature? How does she use nature images to make a point? Note your observations in a sentence or two.

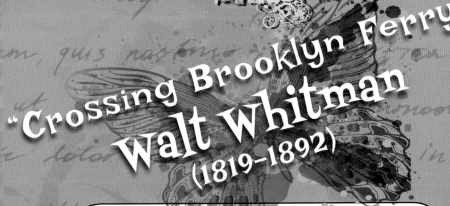

# 6

# "Crossing Brooklyn Ferry"
# Walt Whitman
# (1819–1892)

Walt Whitman had always loved to read. He admired the British Romantic poets, such as John Keats, Lord Byron, William Wordsworth, and Samuel Taylor Coleridge. They had all begun writing in their teens and twenties. Whitman started his career in poetry when he was older. In the beginning lines of his poem, "Song of Myself," he wrote "I, now thirty-seven years old, in perfect health, begin. . . ."

Whitman had a mission to represent the American spirit. His "I" speaker refers to both Whitman himself and every human being. He embraced an American "I," the sense of individualism he witnessed in the new and growing nation. He grew up in the company of farmers and laborers—simple country people. He identified with common working people, his family, friends, and neighbors. He knew that, at the time, this set him apart from other poets.

Whitman lived much of his life near the ocean, and he also lived in the bustling cities of the day. He keenly observed nature and the growing cities of Manhattan and Brooklyn. He kept track of the political and cultural events of the United States. When he lived for many years in Brooklyn, he watched the ships, reveled in the salty air, and smelled the fish and seaweed. He rode the Fulton Ferry across the East River to Manhattan. He talked with the ferrymen.

The contrasts between city and country and between land and sea impressed him deeply. He found strength in opposites in nature and in the world. He had an ability to embrace opposites and find the intersections between land and sea, past and future, city and country.

In his preface to *Leaves of Grass*, he wrote: "The sea is not surer of the shore or the shore of the sea than he is of the fruition of his love and of all perfection and beauty." He felt as close to his work as the sea to the shore. He poured his experience into his poetry so fully that in the final poem of his book *Leaves of Grass*, he wrote: "This is no book/Who touches this touches a man."

Walt Whitman

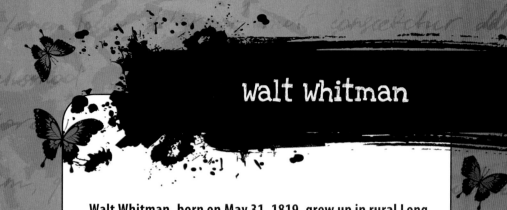

# Walt Whitman

Walt Whitman, born on May 31, 1819, grew up in rural Long Island, New York, second oldest in a working-class family of eight children. He was four when his family moved to Brooklyn, then a town of about seven thousand people. At age twelve, he left school and apprenticed as a printer. For many years, he worked as a journalist in Manhattan and Brooklyn. He founded his own newspaper, *The Long Islander*, in his hometown of Huntington.

By 1850, Whitman had grown more interested in writing poetry than in journalism. In 1855, he used his own money to print the first edition of *Leaves of Grass*. The book, with twelve long poems, did not sell well. But two important nature writers, Ralph Waldo Emerson and Henry David Thoreau, praised it. Emerson and Thoreau were part of a literary movement called transcendentalism. Part of the philosophy and purpose of transcendentalism was to establish a firmer connection to nature. They found different ways to unite with nature. They lived in solitude or turned to farming. Whitman, although not part of the movement, embodied some transcendentalist principles.

In 1873, Whitman suffered a stroke. He sought to heal himself, as he wrote in his journal, "in solitude with Nature—open, voiceless, mystic, far-removed, yet palpable, eloquent Nature."

# "Crossing Brooklyn Ferry"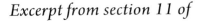

*Flow on, river! flow with the flood-tide, and ebb
with the ebb-tide!*
*Frolic on, crested and scallop-edg'd waves!*
*Gorgeous clouds of the sunset! drench with your
splendor me, or the men and women generations
after me!*
*Cross from shore to shore, countless crowds of
passengers!*
*Stand up, tall masts of Mannahatta! stand up,
beautiful hills of Brooklyn!*
*Throb, baffled and curious brain! throw out
questions and answers!*
*Suspend here and everywhere, eternal float of
solution!*
*Gaze, loving and thirsting eyes, in the house or
street or public assembly!*
*Sound out, voices of young men! loudly and
musically call me by my nighest\* name!*
*Live, old life! play the part that looks back on
the actor or actress!*
*Play the old role, the role that is great or small
according as one makes it!*

Consider, you who peruse me, whether I may not in unknown ways be looking upon you;
Be firm, rail over the river, to support those who lean idly, yet haste with the hasting current;
Fly on, sea-birds! fly sideways, or wheel in large circles high in the air;
Receive the summer sky, you water, and faithfully hold it till all downcast eyes have time to take it from you!
Diverge, fine spokes of light, from the shape of my head, or any one's head, in the sunlit water!
Come on, ships from the lower bay! pass up or down, white-sail'd schooners, sloops, lighters!
Flaunt away, flags of all nations! be duly lower'd at sunset!
Burn high your fires, foundry chimneys! cast black shadows at nightfall! cast red and yellow light over the tops of the houses!

*nighest: nearest

# Summary

In "Crossing Brooklyn Ferry," Whitman rides a ferry at the end of the day with a crowd of other people commuting between Manhattan and Brooklyn. Whitman stands on deck, joyously celebrating all of nature. He watches the panoramic skyline of the growing cities, and he watches the crowds of people on deck. He imagines all the people who lived before him who, although now gone, once crossed the same waters, from shore to shore. He thinks of the countless people who will travel across the same waters after his death. Those people will see the same sights that he is looking at now.

# Explication

At the time Whitman wrote this poem, he rode the ferry often. He wrote about literal ferry rides. However, by invoking past and future human generations, he turns the ferry ride into a symbolic journey. Every image in this poem takes on a heightened symbolism. Traveling across water, from one shore to another, becomes a spiritual journey. It represents the meeting of body and soul, the lifetime of a single person and generations of people, and the fusion of past, present, and future time.

In this section, Whitman exclaims, "Flow on, River!" Next, he describes the countless people who ride the ferry, to cross from shore to shore. It is as if he is saying that people and time also flow on. He is watching the sunset from the boat on the water. When he writes, "Gorgeous clouds of the sunset! drench with your splendor me . . . ," he captures his personal sense of being immersed in the world. But then he wishes "the men and women generations after me!" the same splendor. It does not matter to him whether the sunset washes over him or someone else. Sunset, the ending of a day, is also a daily reminder of time passing. It symbolizes all endings in time. Other people, not yet born, will ride the ferry after Whitman. They will "cross from shore to shore." They will live their lives from birth to death.

"Crossing Brooklyn Ferry" is, in part, a celebration of time passing. Just as Whitman seems to throw open his arms and his senses to all of nature, he embraces the movement of time that will eventually lead to his death. Whitman was very aware of the historical context of his own time. He knew he was living in an exciting and significant era, witnessing the birth of a new country, the building of new cities.

In his time, he embraced the past and the future. He captured his intensely individual experiences, but he also made them universal. He believed that his life was in some ways just like everyone else's. He believed that he was part of something larger than himself, a cyclical wave of birth and death. He describes all of nature—water, sea-birds, and breezes—and extends the experience to all people, from the past, present, and future.

# Style, Technique, and Poetic Devices

Rather than use a narrative structure, Whitman often lists descriptive images, one after another. Whitman writes in free verse, a form of poetry that does not use traditional patterns of rhyme and meter. Free verse can be composed of natural speech. Whitman's lines are unstructured and fragmented. Instead of strict rhyme and meter, he uses rhythm and repetition to establish the music of the poem.

Using a literary device called anaphora, he begins a series of lines with the same word, phrase, or sentence pattern. This makes his poems sound like chants. Run down the list of lines in section 11 of "Crossing Brooklyn Ferry" to discover that almost every line begins with the command form of a verb—Flow on, Frolic on, Gaze, Stand up. . . . These active commands give the poem a dramatic, powerful, and energetic tone. There is nothing indecisive or questioning in Whitman's voice. It is as if he is directing nature and time.

Whitman's use of anaphora allows him to connect unrelated images. The images jump around, but the form remains consistent. This justifies his connection of disparate images and ideas. He can give a command to the river, the clouds, other passengers, and his own brain and eyes. The repeated sentence structure holds these haphazard images together.

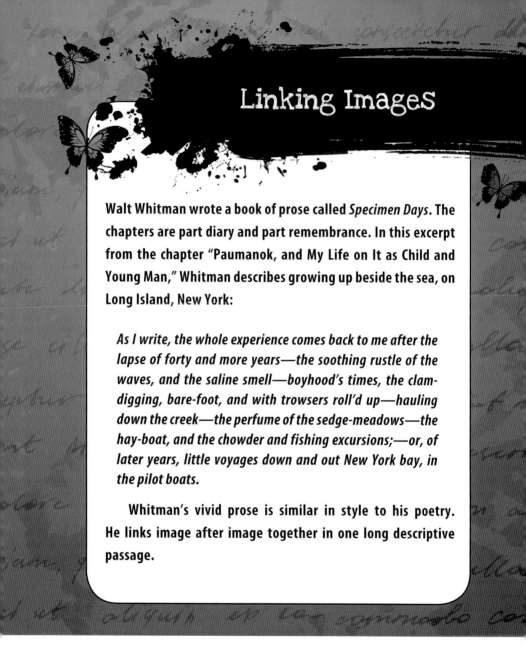

# Linking Images

Walt Whitman wrote a book of prose called *Specimen Days*. The chapters are part diary and part remembrance. In this excerpt from the chapter "Paumanok, and My Life on It as Child and Young Man," Whitman describes growing up beside the sea, on Long Island, New York:

> *As I write, the whole experience comes back to me after the lapse of forty and more years—the soothing rustle of the waves, and the saline smell—boyhood's times, the clam-digging, bare-foot, and with trowsers roll'd up—hauling down the creek—the perfume of the sedge-meadows—the hay-boat, and the chowder and fishing excursions;—or, of later years, little voyages down and out New York bay, in the pilot boats.*

Whitman's vivid prose is similar in style to his poetry. He links image after image together in one long descriptive passage.

The patterns of anaphora create a sense of speech, swelling and building. The anaphoric lines take on the rhythm of a ferry rocking on the waves. The lines sound like the pulsing tides. The ebb and flow of the tides represent generations of people. Within this structure, Whitman's pattern of images come and go, like the tides.

Whitman's repeated images take on greater significance. As he repeats the word *water*, it becomes symbolic, not just a liquid element but a force of life. He uses water imagery to feel unity with other people. In section 3 of "Crossing Brooklyn Ferry," he writes: "Just as you feel when you look on the river and sky, so I felt;/Just as any of you is one of a living crowd, I was one of a crowd." Using the ocean as a metaphor, Whitman is able to suggest that all individuals are connected with each other and with nature.

# Thematic Relevance

In his 1855 preface to *Leaves of Grass*, Walt Whitman wrote: "What do you think is the grandeur of storms and dismemberments and the deadliest battles and wrecks and the wildest fury of the elements and the power of the sea and the motion of nature and the throes of human desires and dignity and hate and love?" Even in his prose, he links image after image of the ocean.

His book contains many images of land. However, as he states in the poem "In Cabin'd Ships at Sea," *Leaves of Grass* is "ocean's poem," and the poems are full of "liquid-flowing syllables." Water is a major symbol in Whitman's poems. The sea recurs frequently.

Whitman even compared his poetic style to the ocean. Of his poetry, he told his friend Horace Traubel, who published Whitman's words in *Walt Whitman in Camden*,

"Its verses are the liquid, billowy waves, ever rising and falling, perhaps sunny and smooth, perhaps wild with storm, always moving, always alike in their nature as rolling waves. . . ."

Whitman often wrote about the intersection between land and sea. He was fascinated with the places where they meet. Land can mean life, water death, and vice versa. Things from land get thrown into the water; debris from the water washes up on land. There is an exchange, but they never fully merge. In some poems, Whitman stands on the shore watching the water. In other poems, he sails on the water, looking at the land.

Whitman often crossed water to get from one land point to another. On this journey, described in "Crossing Brooklyn Ferry," written in 1856, Whitman feels a deep sense of unity with others, even people of the future. In a hundred years, he says, and a hundred years after that, other ferry passengers, like him, "Will enjoy the sunset, the pouring in of the flood-tide, the falling back to the sea of the ebb-tide."

Whitman reprinted *Leaves of Grass* many times, adding new poems to each edition. The final "Death-Bed" version, published in 1892, contains almost four hundred poems. During his lifetime, some, but not all, of his readers saw his greatness. They called him America's poet and the first poet of democracy. After his death, the significance of Whitman's work grew when new poets promoted him.

# Further Study Questions

**Recall Questions**

    1. What is anaphora?

    2. How does anaphora create the tone in Whitman's poem?

    3. What is a line in the poem that illustrates the theme of time?

**Ponder Further**

    4. Both Walt Whitman's poem and Elizabeth Barrett Browning's take place near the ocean. Compare the two poems.

    5. Online or in the library, find and read another selection of sea imagery from Whitman's *Leaves of Grass*, such as in "Song of Myself." Using what you learned in this chapter, analyze this brief section. How does Whitman use the sea as a metaphor? How can you recognize Whitman's style in the lines?

# "Make Me a Picture of the Sun"
# Emily Dickinson
## (1830–1886)

Emily Dickinson wrote many poems about the sun's movement. She felt drawn to the sun during its moments of intense change—sunrise and sunset. "I'll tell you how the sun rose/A ribbon at a time," she wrote in one playful poem. Fascinated by the human inability to measure nature, she attempts to capture the qualities of light as it quickly slips away. "Bring me the sunset in a cup," she humorously commands.

The speed of nature's changes scared her. Changing light intensified her emotions. Dickinson associated it with grief, loss, sadness, fear, and death. In one well-known poem, she wrote: "There's a certain slant of light,/

On winter afternoons,/That oppresses, like the weight/ Of cathedral tunes." The sunset seems to come as a daily surprise: "The day came slow, till five o'clock,/Then sprang before the hills/Like hindered rubies, or the light/A sudden musket spills." When the sun goes away, it leaves the world in fearful darkness, symbolizing death and mortality. Nature's changes could also symbolize her psychological state. In "Time and Eternity," she wrote: "How softly sinks his trembling sun/In human nature's west!"

Dickinson greatly admired the poetry of Elizabeth Barrett Browning. Allegedly, she hung a portrait of Barrett Browning on the wall of her room. Dickinson also had an interest in visual art. Like many thinkers of the time, she read Ralph Waldo Emerson's essay "Nature." Dickinson also considered his ideas. However, while Emerson felt united with nature, Dickinson often seemed startled by nature in her poems—fascinated, delighted, a close observer, and in awe, but never really one with nature. Rather, she often seemed struck by nature's indifference to humanity.

## Summary

In this playful poem, the speaker requests a picture of the sun. She wants to hang it on her bedroom wall. That way, she can look at the picture inside the way she looks at the sun in the sky. Inside, she can pretend she is warm and it is day. She can imagine that a cheerful robin chirps at night. At the poem's end, and in the speaker's game of pretend, things in

# Make Me a Picture of the Sun
## (Poem #188)

Make me a picture of the sun—
So I can hang it in my room—
And make believe I'm getting warm
When others call it "Day"!

Draw me a Robin—on a stem—
So I am hearing him, I'll dream,
And when the Orchards stop their tune—
Put my pretense*—away—

Say if it's really—warm at noon—
Whether it's Buttercups—that "skim"—
Or Butterflies—that "bloom"?
Then—skip—the frost—upon the lea*—
And skip the Russet*—on the tree—
Let's play those—never come!

*pretense: pretending; the act of make-believe

*lea: an open, grassy field or meadow

*Russet: a reddish orange color

nature become even more confused. Living creatures lose their natural order. A butterfly blooms. A flower flies. In her world, it is always summer. Winter never comes.

# Explication

At first, "Make Me a Picture of the Sun" seems to address the speaker's desire to copy and reinvent nature. In the end, the poem seems to be about the speaker's desire to live in the world of her imagination rather than in the real world of nature. As the speaker conveys a childlike longing for pretty pictures, the poet conveys an adult tendency to deny fears of life's changes.

Dickinson's speaker is the created persona of a child. The speaker plays a child's game of pretend or make-believe. In a playful voice, she makes commands. Children love to order other people around. "Make me a picture of the sun" and "Draw me a Robin," she demands. She desires art to celebrate nature and bring it inside. However, she also wants to escape the realities of life. The speaker knows that, with a picture of the sun, she can only pretend to be warm. And if she has a picture of a robin, she can only imagine she hears it singing. She wants to live in the world of her creative imagination.

The speaker grows more aware of the absurdity of her desires when she suggests that butterflies can bloom and flowers fly. Nature is mixed up. But she does not want the

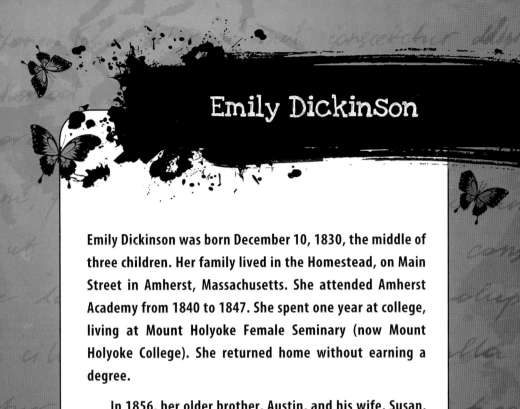

# Emily Dickinson

Emily Dickinson was born December 10, 1830, the middle of three children. Her family lived in the Homestead, on Main Street in Amherst, Massachusetts. She attended Amherst Academy from 1840 to 1847. She spent one year at college, living at Mount Holyoke Female Seminary (now Mount Holyoke College). She returned home without earning a degree.

In 1856, her older brother, Austin, and his wife, Susan, moved next door, to the house called the Evergreens. Their home was a social hub. Susan had been Dickinson's school friend, and Emily attended some of their parties and dinners. She was very shy, however. As she grew older, she retreated into reclusiveness. She kept in touch by sending daily notes over to the Evergreens.

Dickinson lived the rest of her life in the Homestead with her younger sister, Lavinia. Neither of them married. They kept house and cared for their parents. Dickinson spent much of her time writing poems. She wrote letters to other people, too. In 1862, she sent Thomas Wentworth Higginson, an *Atlantic Monthly* contributor, four of her poems. They corresponded for the rest of her life.

real world, she wants a representation. Her paintings will never come to life. Images in art never change. That is what the speaker wants. The bird will never fly away. The sun will never rise or set. Her picture on the wall will shine at night, allowing her to deny her fears of darkness.

The speaker sounds powerful, making demands, but if she is requesting pictures, it means she will not paint them herself. Does she lack an artist's ability to interpret nature for herself? Dickinson writes the poem, but her speaker cannot create art. In truth, the child-speaker lacks power. She has no control over nature. No one does. Perhaps it means the poet has no control over her own fears.

Inside her room, with her pretend sun, robin, and orchard, she can pretend that it is never night, never cold, and never winter. "Let's play those—never come," she says about frost and fall colors in the last line. The speaker does not want day to end. The poet does not want life to end. She wants to pretend nature never changes and death does not exist. In pretending it could be so, Dickinson affirms her keen awareness of the inevitability of both.

# Style, Technique, & Poetic Devices

Dickinson often created personas. Her "I" speakers are not herself. This allowed her to infuse her writing style with a light humor. Dickinson's speakers reveal profound truths, mainly in the poems' interpretation. The speakers do not always sound as if they genuinely speak from the heart. Using a child persona allows Dickinson to create a playful tone and a sense of innocence. The speaker might not understand her own game of pretense as much as the reader does.

With its fourteen lines, "Make Me a Picture of the Sun" is a simple sonnet. Dickinson uses a loose rhyme scheme of *aaab/cccb/ded/ffe*. The words at the end of each line are called slant rhymes. For example, the words *room* and *warm* are not perfect rhymes, but they sound close. The words *stem* and *dream* share the *m*-consonant. Although they are not exact rhymes, they sound similar enough to create the poem's music.

The sonnet has its turning point in a stanza break, the space between lines 8 and 9. As her speaker plays a game of pretend, she promises to put her "pretense" away. In fact, her pretending grows. Line 9 begins with another request, "Say if it's really. . . ." This time, she wants to pretend her pretending is real. Her make-believe grows even more unrealistic.

Throughout the poem, Dickinson uses simple words. Although the speaker's tone is childlike, there is a sense that the poet is jesting, speaking tongue in cheek. The simplicity of her innocent language contrasts with the enormity of her themes—the universe, cosmos, great art, seasonal changes, time, and death.

# Thematic Relevance

Dickinson published fewer than twelve poems in her lifetime. When she died, on May 15, 1886, her sister Lavinia found 1,700 poems she had written. The first publishers to organize Dickinson's poems tried to sort them into thematic categories, such as nature, beauty, love, life, death, time, and eternity. They soon found the task impossible. No poem is only on one theme. Dickinson's nature poems are also about time, eternity, death, and life. Some poems contain all her main themes.

Dickinson had an intimate relationship with nature. She collected and studied flowers. She was fascinated with nature's small creatures: bees, snakes, spiders, flies, and birds. In many poems, she captures nature's movement. Animals are there, then gone. Birds fly off. Snakes disappear. The wind blows. Seasons come and go. Many of Dickinson's nature poems take place outside.

However, as in "Make Me a Picture of the Sun," Dickinson also brought nature inside. Some critics have suggested that she tried to gain control over her life by rejecting nature. She went upstairs to her bedroom, closed the door, and wrote at her small desk. She often uses nature imagery as metaphors for the human nature inside her. "Have you got a brook in your little heart?" she asks in one poem. In another poem, she invites a season into her room: "Oh, March, come right upstairs with me,/I have so much to tell!"

Dickinson is now considered by some to be one of the best lyric poets ever. There has been much speculation about her life. Critics have observed that she lived life in her mind rather than in society. As an introvert, she spent a great deal of time alone in her room. In a preface to her poems, her friend and publisher Thomas Wentworth Higginson described Emily Dickinson as "literally spending years without setting her foot beyond the doorstep, and many more years during which her walks were strictly limited to her father's grounds. . . ." Maybe the inner world of her imagination was as large as the outer natural world.

# Further Study Questions

## Recall Questions

1. What is slant rhyme? Use an example from the poem to define the device.

2. What is one reason why Emily Dickinson seemed fascinated with sunrises and sunsets?

3. What happens in lines 9 to 11?

**Ponder Further**

4. The explication offers one interpretation of the poem. What is another way to interpret the speaker's request for a picture of the sun?

5. The yard surrounding Dickinson's home was filled with flower gardens. You can read about the property on the Web site *Emily Dickinson Museum*. How do you think Dickinson's home environment helped make her the kind of nature poet that she was?

# "Sympathy"
# Paul Laurence Dunbar
# (1872–1906)

At Ohio Central High School, in Dayton, Ohio, Paul Laurence Dunbar was class president, president of the literary club, and editor of the school newspaper. He was also the only African-American student in his class. The Civil War may have ended in 1865, but racial unrest still gripped the country, especially in the South. However, even in Ohio—a northern state—African Americans struggled to find opportunities.

When Dunbar graduated in 1890, he was an intelligent and skilled writer. But no one would hire him for higher-level work. He took a job as an elevator operator at the Callahan Building in Dayton, Ohio. On the side, he wrote articles for newspapers and magazines. He wrote poems as he drove the elevator car up and down. When he was twenty-one, he paid his own money to self-publish his first book, *Oak and Ivy*. He sold copies to people riding in his elevator. People in Dayton started to know him as a poet. Word spread about his talents.

In 1893, he was invited to read his poetry at the World's Fair in Chicago. There, Dunbar met civil rights leader Frederick Douglass. In 1895, Dunbar's second book, *Majors and Minors,* was published. William Dean Howells, an influential critic and novelist, reviewed the book for *Harper's Weekly*, praising Dunbar's work. Dunbar shot to instant fame. A New York publisher, Dodd, Mead and Co., combined Dunbar's first two books and printed his poems in *Lyrics of Lowly Life* in 1896. Howells wrote the introduction. Soon, national and international readers read Dunbar's poetry. As his fame grew, he became a voice for African Americans. He became friends with others doing the same work, such as Booker T. Washington, W. E. B. DuBois, and Charles Chestnut.

Dunbar had two distinct writing styles. In one of these distinct writing styles, he wrote poems in literary English, in the style of Victorian lyric poetry. In a somber, serious tone, he wrote about love and hope, death and loss. In some poems, he addresses issues of race, oppression, and slavery, such as "We Wear the Mask," "Sympathy," and

Paul Laurence Dunbar

"The Haunted Tree." He expresses the pain of slavery in "Ode to Ethiopia":

> *O Mother Race! to thee I bring*
> *This pledge of faith unwavering,*
> *This tribute to thy glory.*
> *I know the pangs which thou didst feel,*
> *When Slavery crushed thee with its heel,*
> *With thy dear blood all gory.*

Dunbar's other writing style was livelier and more lighthearted. He composed these poems using the common, everyday speech, or dialect, of African Americans. Many of his dialect poems describe the full, bustling daily life of people around him and the families he grew up with. He describes the parties, spelling bees, and church services of small communities. The first lines of "Song of Summer" describe a beautiful day:

> *Dis is gospel weathah sho'—*
> *Hills is sawt o' hazy.*
> *Meddahs level ez a flo'*
> *Callin' to de lazy.*

When Dunbar used dialect, some critics accused him of stereotyping African Americans. They thought that his cheerful dialect poems did not tell the truth about the misery, poverty, and injustice of African-American life. But other critics praised him for portraying true African-American culture. They called dialect Dunbar's real poetic

# Sympathy

I know what the caged bird feels, alas!
　　When the sun is bright on the upland slopes;
When the wind stirs soft through the springing grass,
And the river flows like a stream of glass;
　　When the first bird sings and the first bud opes*,
And the faint perfume from its chalice* steals—
I know what the caged bird feels!

I know why the caged bird beats his wing
　　Till its blood is red on the cruel bars;
For he must fly back to his perch and cling
When he fain* would be on the bough a-swing;
　　And a pain still throbs in the old, old scars
And they pulse again with a keener sting—
I know why he beats his wing!

I know why the caged bird sings, ah me,
　　When his wing is bruised and his bosom sore,—
When he beats his bars and he would be free;
It is not a carol of joy or glee,
　　But a prayer that he sends from his heart's deep core,
But a plea, that upward to Heaven he flings—
I know why the caged bird sings!

*opes: short for opens

*chalice: cup

*fain: obliged or required, compelled, as if forced

voice. Both the criticism and the praise baffled Dunbar. He grew up hearing his parents' songs and stories about plantation life. Dialect was a huge part of his heritage. However, he also grew up studying academic literature. His influences included such poets as William Wordsworth; Samuel Taylor Coleridge; Percy Shelley; and Alfred, Lord Tennyson. Dunbar wrote well in both styles. He wrote more often in literary English. He grew tired of people requesting poems in dialect.

## Summary

In this poem, the speaker has a revelation. "I know!" he exclaims. From beginning to end, he asserts his knowledge gained from sympathizing with a caged bird. He does not give any specifics of his personal circumstances. He leaves unsaid any reasons why he relates to the caged bird. He makes it clear in the first line with the word "Alas!" that his identification with the caged bird is painful.

First, the speaker looks out at the natural world that the bird has lost—the beautiful, idyllic freedom of sipping from flowers and flying in a sunny sky. Next, he focuses on life in the cage. The bird has suffered injury trying to escape. Last, he goes inside the heart of the bird itself. He reveals that he knows why the bird sings. The caged bird sings because it cries out in prayer.

# Explication

The speaker in "Sympathy" never states why the caged bird represents his circumstances. He provides no personal or historic events to give the poem context. Many critics, knowing Dunbar's biography, believe the caged bird stands for the struggles of African Americans. Dunbar's lack of specific context makes the poem rich, evocative, and timeless. "Sympathy" can speak to anyone who feels deeply oppressed. Even though the speaker's identification with the bird is painful, he moves from despair to hope.

Like the bird, the speaker finds a source of poetic expression that could help him triumph over oppression. The poet achieves this by describing three stages of personal growth. The bird is first passive, then is active but self-destructive, and, finally, acts in a positive way. This poem is powerful not only because the speaker identifies with the pain of the caged bird but because the speaker is inspired by the bird's ability to change and grow.

The stanzas progress in order. In the first one, the speaker knows how the caged bird feels. He describes the beauty that the bird misses. He longs for the natural life the bird was born to live. He feels anger that the bird is not living outdoors and remorse over its wasted potential. At this point, there is no mention of the cage. The bird and the speaker helplessly look outside to the natural world the bird has been denied.

In the second stanza, the bird takes action. It beats its wing. However, by thrashing against the bars of the cage, it only hurts itself. The bird no longer looks out to nature. It tries to conquer the cage with physical strength. When it gives up and passively flies back to sit on its perch, it feels a moment of defeat. However, in line 13, its scars "pulse again with a keener sting." The bird refuses to give up. It prepares to act again.

In the third stanza, the bird sings. It sends its song into the air. The cage has not suppressed its natural ability to sing, which is both a form of artistic expression and an active way to seek help. The bird has transformed pain into song. The speaker interprets the birdsong as a cry for help and a prayer. Dunbar implies that, even in prison, the bird has found a small freedom. Dunbar does not give his poem a fourth stanza with a sweet ending. He does not tie the poem up neatly. The bird is not yet free. Its cries for help have not yet been answered. However, that the bird found its voice represents triumph. If the bird can sing, there is the possibility of change.

# Style, Technique & Poetic Devices

"Sympathy" is an extended metaphor, meaning it is longer than a standard metaphor which may only be one line. For the entire poem, Dunbar uses the metaphor, as the speaker compares himself to the caged bird. The bird represents the

# Dialect

Dunbar wrote some poems in literary English, the style of much Victorian lyric poetry. He wrote other poems in the dialect, everyday speech patterns and vocabulary, of African Americans. Read excerpts of four other nature poems by Paul Laurence Dunbar. Compare the two writing styles—dialect and literary English.

| Dialect | Literary English |
| :---: | :---: |
| A Corn-Song | A Starry Night |
| Oh, we hoe de co'n<br>Since de ehly mo'n<br>Now de sinkin' sun<br>Says de day is done. | A cloud fell down from the heavens,<br>And broke on the mountain's brow;<br>It scattered the dusky fragments<br>All over the vale below. |
| The Plantation Child's Lullaby | The Lily of the Valley |
| Wintah time hit comin'<br>Stealin' thoo de night;<br>Wake up in the mo'nin'<br>Evah t'ing is white; | Sweetest of the flowers a-blooming<br>In the fragrant vernal days<br>Is the Lily of the Valley<br>With its soft, retiring ways. |

speaker's struggle to be free from oppression. The speaker implies that he is like the bird. His circumstances are like a cage. The metaphor of a caged bird describes the speaker's emotional intensity.

Dunbar writes three separate stanzas. He encloses each one by repeating the first and last lines. It is as if each stanza were a cage, containing the speaker's thoughts. In that way, the poet's own ability to express himself is caged. This idea is emphasized in his line lengths. The first six lines of each stanza contain four feet, called a tetrameter. The last lines of each stanza are in trimeter, meaning they have only three beats. The meter is shortened, as if to represent that the speaker's speech is cut off. Much is left unsaid.

Dunbar uses short words. Most have only one syllable. This gives the poem melody and rhythm. It also gives it a blunt and direct simplicity. His word choices are full of assonance, words that share internal vowel sounds, and consonance, words that share internal or ending consonant sounds. In the first stanza, the *s*-sound echoes in *feels* and *alas* and the *p*-sound in *upland* and *slopes*. In the second stanza, a *d*-sound thrums in *caged, bird, blood,* and *red.* In the third stanza, the long *e*-sound in *me, beats, free, glee, deep,* and *plea* begins to sound triumphant and exuberant. Those are just some examples! You can find many more examples of assonance and consonance. In one way, this poem is Paul Laurence Dunbar's birdsong. His monosyllabic words are like musical notes.

# Thematic Relevance

Dunbar became one of the first African Americans to receive recognition as a poet in the United States. Many other African Americans were writing at the time, but Dunbar was considered the most well-known African-American author. In the 1898 introduction to *Lyrics of Lowly Life*, William Dean Howells wrote: "So far as I could remember, Paul Dunbar was the only man of pure African blood and of American civilization to feel the negro life aesthetically and express it lyrically." Howells called Dunbar the first African-American poet. Howells did Dunbar a favor when he praised the poet. However, Howells also singled Dunbar out. The review placed more attention on Dunbar's dialect poems than his poems in standard or literary English. As pleased as Dunbar was by the positive review, the comments put pressure on him to write in dialect.

In his short life, he wrote a dozen books of poetry, four books of short stories, five novels, a play, and song lyrics. Critics praised Dunbar's work for its accurate portrayal of African-American life. Dunbar included "Sympathy" in his book *Lyrics of the Hearthside*, published in 1899. Many readers interpret "Sympathy" as a metaphor for the repression of slavery. Some readers think it could also represent Dunbar's situation as an African-American artist, writing in a time of deep racial prejudice.

Paul Laurence Dunbar was born on June 27, 1872, in Dayton, Ohio, less than a decade after Abraham Lincoln issued the Emancipation Proclamation. Dunbar's parents were both former slaves. They were poor and struggled to support a family. His mother, Matilda, especially encouraged her son to succeed. She put a priority on his schoolwork.

Dunbar was friends with his high school classmate Orville Wright. As a student, Wright began a printing press. Dunbar started the *Dayton Tattler*, the city's first African-American newspaper. Wright printed it. After graduation, Dunbar asked Wright to print his book, but Wright lacked the equipment to bind a book's spine. Wright suggested that Dunbar print *Oak and Ivy* at the United Brethren publishing house in downtown Dayton.

In 1898, Dunbar married writer Alice Ruth Moore. His book *Lyrics of Lowly Life* appeared in 1896. Two more books, *Lyrics of the Hearthside* and *Poems of Cabin and Field*, were both published in 1899. In 1900, Dunbar contracted tuberculosis. He used alcohol to numb the symptoms. This led to public and private violent rages. By 1902, his marriage had failed and his health was worse. He moved back to his mother's home in Dayton, Ohio. He died there on February 9, 1906. He was thirty-three years old.

Dunbar inspired Harlem Renaissance authors, such as Langston Hughes and Zora Neale Hurston, as well as the famous modern writer Maya Angelou. Angelou connected with Dunbar's poem so much that she wrote a poem of her own called "Caged Bird" and titled her autobiography *I Know Why the Caged Bird Sings*, published in 1969.

# Further Study Questions

### Recall Questions

1. What is the main idea of the second stanza of "Sympathy"?

2. Most lines are in four-beat lines called tetrameter. What is the rhythm in the last line of each stanza?

3. How does Dunbar convince readers to understand how the speaker felt? What poetic techniques does Dunbar use to help shape a reader's response?

### Ponder Further

4. How does historical context and biographical information about Paul Laurence Dunbar's life and times help readers to interpret "Sympathy"?

5. Dunbar's poetry inspired twentieth-century authors who came after him, especially Langston Hughes (1902–1967). Hughes was part of the literary movement called the Harlem Renaissance. In the library, research the Harlem Renaissance. In a paragraph, describe the period.

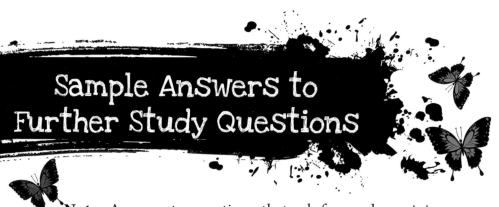

# Sample Answers to Further Study Questions

**Note:** Answers to questions that ask for reader opinions will vary. There is no one correct answer. Responses should, however, demonstrate a close reading of texts.

## CHAPTER 1: "To the Moon"
### Charlotte Turner Smith (1749–1806)

1. For such a short poem, the sonnet has many formal elements. A sonnet must contain rhyming quatrains or couplets, often written in iambic pentameter. The speaker makes an argument. The topic often changes in the middle.

2. Women were not encouraged to write about their personal feelings. They were expected to conceal them.

3. She wants her life to end quickly because she suffers while she is alive.

4. When the speaker asks, "But can they peace to this sad breast restore . . . ," she no longer describes a pretty landscape that she loves. She asks whether the landscape of her childhood can heal emotional pain. It is a rhetorical question. For the speaker, the answer is no. She feels connected to nature but also apart from it.

5. In gothic stories, a main character faces a test, usually alone in a strange, terrifying landscape. Sometimes, it seems like nature is out to get the character. You don't know whether the person is paranoid or the fears are real. Because gothic literature is psychological, nature can be supernatural, almost dreamlike. Examples of natural settings are secret gardens, a rocky shore, narrow roads, ruined mansions, storms, fallen trees, trees scratching at windows, and moaning wind.

## CHAPTER 2: "Lines Written in Early Spring" William Wordsworth (1770–1850)

1. The main idea is that human beings are connected to nature.

2. He interpreted the meaning of nature for readers.

/     /     /

3. What MAN has MADE of MAN.

4. John Clare's speaker disturbs a field by stumbling around in it. In the end, he still knows nothing about nature. Wordsworth's speaker, however, observes a scene in nature without touching it at all. In the end, he has a profound realization about nature. Clare and Wordsworth convey the same message: humans affect nature and vice versa. Clare's speaker, a created persona, does not understand his impact on nature. Wordsworth's speaker, himself, is

composed and respectful. He is aware of his connection to nature, but he does not describe the way his physical presence could have affected the grove.

5. Emerson, like Wordsworth, also learns by observing nature. His poems teach his readers what he learns. In some ways, Emerson and Wordsworth believe nature is "smarter" than humanity. In "Water," Emerson says that "[t]he Water understands Civilization well." In "Berrying," the berry vines speak their wisdom. In "April," nature knows more than a book ever will.

## CHAPTER 3: "Frost at Midnight"
**Samuel Taylor Coleridge (1772–1834)**

1. The speaker is in his cottage at night, near a fireplace, with his sleeping child.

2. Coleridge records his thoughts. He starts out unknowing and, by talking out a problem, reaches an important conclusion.

3. Coleridge sat in a classroom but did not focus on the studies. Instead, he was pulled outside by a person at the window. The experience is significant because he was intensely restless and bored inside and was unable to reach the object of his fascination outside. It is significant because he still feels that way as an adult sometimes.

4. The chart shows examples. Your observations might be different!

| "Lines Written in Early Spring" | "Frost at Midnight" |
|---|---|
| Short poem | Long poem |
| speaker sits outside, observes nature | speaker sits inside, thinks about nature |
| uses an impersonal rational tone | uses a relaxed, private tone |
| discusses nature vs. humanity | discusses nature and childhood |
| observations are general— "a thousand blended notes" | observations are specific— "the owlet's cry" |
| poem ends on a statement | poem ends on an image |
| message has a negative outlook | message has a positive outlook |

**Comparison Comments:** Both poems are meditations on nature. Each poet reflects on a human problem and the role that nature plays in resolving it. Coleridge comes to a positive resolution for a single person, his child. Wordsworth ends on a note of doom for all of humanity!

5. The speaker in "Frost at Midnight" sits inside by a fire. The harsh weather of winter limits his activities. In winter, people think about survival. Winter is linked to darkness and even death because days are short. The speaker in "Stopping by Woods on a Snowy Evening," by Robert Frost, is alone in a woods during a snowfall. In summer, he would have noticed a woods filled with life, animals, and growing plants.

### CHAPTER 4: "The Mouse's Nest"
### John Clare (1793–1864)

1. The nest is hidden in the hay or grass somewhere on a large open field. The location is important because the man does not see the nest until he steps on it.

2. Clare leaves the story unfinished but closes the form with rhyme and imagery.

3. When he keeps walking, he assumes the mouse will be fine.

4. I see the speaker as a peasant, like Clare himself. He is younger, in his teens maybe. He is not cruel but simple, clumsy but curious. He kicks at a ball of grass like any kid would. He wants to catch a bird, and he wonders about life. He is not out observing nature. Although he is curious, he does not seem able to learn. When he leaves the mouse, the rhyme scheme goes back to the beginning. He is no smarter than he was before he kicked her.

5. The poem's speaker is probably more changed than he thinks he is. He does not realize how much his life is like the mouse's life.

   *As fast as I could I ran inside my house*
   *I could not shake the feeling I was too much like the*
   *mouse.*

## CHAPTER 5: "A Sea-Side Walk"
### Elizabeth Barrett Browning (1806–1861)

1. She says the "grey" water "swang in its moon-taught way," but the moon does not really teach the ocean. Tides happen naturally.

2. She heard silence. The silence seemed to breathe. The silence was like a sound. It made her feel connected to nature. She felt nature's "heart."

3. Rhyme: *aabbacc*. Meter: The first and last line of every stanza is a three-beat line. The middle lines have five beats.

4. Walking on a sandy shore is like not being part of either ocean or land but being touched by both. A few steps to either side, and the speaker would be in the water or walking on firmer ground. She might feel the ocean's spray. Loose sand is hard to walk on. Dusk, she says, is a "time of doubt," with a lifelike beauty. A few minutes before is day, and a few minutes later is night. The speaker can exist only temporarily within the poem's time and setting. Pretty soon it will be dark. She will go home.

5. In "Sonnet XXXII," the first line, "The first time that the sun rose on thine oath . . .," demonstrates how she uses nature's way of showing time, like she does in "A Sea-Side Walk." When the sun rises, it is the first day after someone says he loves her. She says, "I looked forward to the moon." She wants it to be night again, opposite of day. In the

poem, the speaker doubts she is worthy of love. Maybe at night she wants to hide. After the first two lines, she does not use nature imagery again. In many of the sonnets, she uses only a little nature imagery. The most important theme is love, not nature.

## CHAPTER 6: "Crossing Brooklyn Ferry" Walt Whitman (1819–1892)

1. Anaphora means that the poet repeated the same words or phrases at the beginning of a series of lines or sentences.

2. Anaphora makes Whitman's lines dramatic. They sound like chanting.

3. *Gorgeous clouds of the sunset! drench with your splendor me, or the men and women generations after me!*

4. Whitman rides on a ferry; Barrett Browning's speaker walks on shore. Both deal with how human beings interact with nature. Both speakers have intense, present-moment experiences of nature. Whitman's poem is more external. He calls out to nature and people. Barrett Browning's poem is internal. She has a deep experience of how she is connected to nature. Whitman tries to convince people to pay more attention to nature. Barrett Browning suggests that people don't know how to pay attention to nature.

5. In one part of "Song of Myself," Whitman describes the sea. His style is similar to "Crossing Brooklyn Ferry." He begins three lines with the same word, *sea*, and phrase structure, sea of something. The excerpt conveys Whitman's themes of feeling united with nature and the passage of time. About the sea, he says, "I am integral with you. . . ." Nature, including the sea, is where people are born and also where they die. He adds, "I too am of one phase and of all phases."

## CHAPTER 7: "Make Me a Picture of the Sun"
### Emily Dickinson (1830–1886)

1. The words *noon* and *bloom* are slant rhymes. They sound close, but they are not perfect rhymes.

2. Those times of day happen so quickly. They represent how fast time goes and how quickly life passes.

3. The speaker creates fantastical images of nature in her game of make-believe. Anything can happen in her mind, so she might as well pretend that butterflies can bloom and buttercups skim through the air.

4. A child's happiest moments might be playing in the sun. When she goes inside, she wants to bring part of nature with her. Her request means she is already trying to preserve her memories of spending time in nature. Maybe the poem expresses her desire for a summer day to last so that night and winter will not come. Like Wordsworth,

maybe she simply wants to remember her childhood experiences in nature. It could be more than that, too. She wants to reverse nature. She wants control over the sun, rather than the sun having power over her.

5. Dickinson's nature poems, like John Clare's, focus on small things—on birds, flowers, bugs, snakes, and blades of grass. She looked very closely at things hidden in ordinary backyards rather than, for example, a poet like William Wordsworth, who traveled and saw mountains and valleys.

## CHAPTER 8: "Sympathy"
### Paul Laurence Dunbar (1872–1906)

1. The bird beat its wings against the bars but did not get free.

2. Three-beat lines, called trimeter.

3. Dunbar uses an extended metaphor. The speaker identifies with a caged bird. That makes the reader identify with the caged bird, too. The reader knows how the bird might feel, so the reader also knows how the speaker feels—trapped, helpless, and stifled.

4. Dunbar lived in a time when African Americans were supposed to be free, but they had few opportunities and were discriminated against. When Dunbar wrote this poem, African Americans struggled to assume the freedoms the country claimed to give them. African

Americans did not have equal rights. They could not speak out. It must have been emotionally painful. "Sympathy" expresses more emotional and physical pain than intellectual issues.

5. After World War I, in the 1920s, many African Americans moved to New York City. The Harlem Renaissance was a cultural movement. It was a time of artistic expression, celebrating African-American culture.

# Glossary

**anaphora**—A literary device in which a series of lines begins with a repeated word, phrase, or sentence pattern.

**assonance**—When two or more words share internal vowel sounds (awake/maid).

**ballad**—A poem that includes elements of songs and folktales.

**consonance**—When two or more words share internal or ending consonant sounds (broke/thick).

**couplet**—A pair of end-rhymed lines.

**dialect**—The everyday speech patterns and vocabulary of a specific group of people and usually from a specific geographical area.

**end rhyme**—A pattern made when the last word of a line of poetry sounds the same as the last word in other lines of the same poem.

**explication**—A detailed explanation of a text; a theory, analysis, or interpretation that explains meaning.

**foot**—A rhythmic unit, also called an iamb, of one unstressed and one stressed syllable.

**free verse**—Poetic lines written without a traditional or set pattern of rhyme and meter.

**iambic**—A metrical foot, a poetic rhythm consisting of an unstressed syllable followed by a stressed syllable.

**melancholy**—A deep and long-lasting sadness.

**metaphor**—A figure of speech in which a word is compared to another to suggest similarity between them.

**meter**—The measure of rhythm in a line of poetry; a pattern of stressed and unstressed syllables in a line.

**pentameter**—A line of verse with a meter of five stressed beats.

**persona**—A dramatic character, different from the author, who is the speaker of a poem.

**personification**—A literary device in which human attributes are applied to inanimate objects.

**quatrain**—A stanza of four lines, usually with alternating end rhymes, *abab*.

**rhyme**—A pattern made when two or more words sound identical except for their first letters or syllables (bell/sell/seashell).

**rhyme scheme**—A formal pattern of rhymes in a stanza or poem; noted by letters, pairs of rhyming lines might show a rhyme scheme of *aabb* while alternating rhyming lines might show a rhyme scheme of *abab*, etc.

**simile**—A figure of speech in which two things are compared using the words *like* or *as*.

**slant rhyme**—Words that share some but not all vowel or consonant sounds.

**stanza**—A grouping of lines in a poem, often separated by a line space, similar to a paragraph in prose writing.

**symbolism**—A image that represents or stands for another quality or meaning; also a late-nineteenth-century movement in French art and literature in which objects had symbolic meaning.

# Further Reading

## Books

Andronik, Catherine M. *Wildly Romantic: The English Romantic Poets—The Mad, the Bad, the Dangerous.* New York: Henry Holt and Co., 2007.

Dickinson, Emily. *My Letter to the World and Other Poems.* Toronto: KCP Poetry, 2008.

Mussari, Mark. *Poetry.* New York: Marshall Cavendish Benchmark, 2011.

Pockell, Leslie, ed. *100 Essential American Poems.* New York: Thomas Dunne Books, 2009.

## Internet Addresses

**Poets.org: Nature Poems**
<http://www.poets.org/viewmedia.php/prmMID/5882>

**PoemHunter.com: Nature Poems**
<http://www.poemhunter.com/poems/nature/>

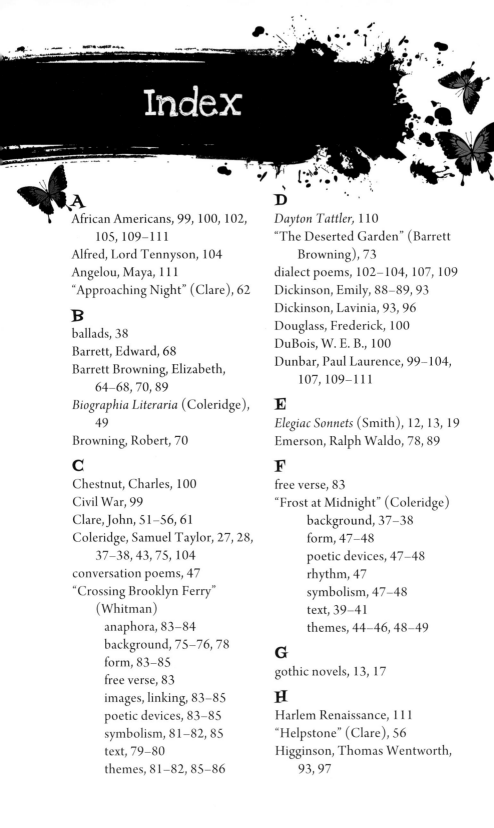

# Index